KASHMIR IS FREE

Attention Authors

'We Convert Fighters into Writers'. That's the motto of Manas Publications since more than four decades. Our message to the world is that India can win the battle not only by the bullet but also by the pen. There is no dearth of intellectuals in our country, but their knowledge is confined to them only. No sincere effort has been made by any other publisher to channelise their knowledge in national interest. That is why the talent of a large number of intellectuals remains latent. An author transforms his knowledge into a manuscript, and it is our job to spread his/her knowledge by converting it into a beautiful book. For over four decades, Manas has been motivating the intellectuals by publishing their manuscripts and would like to publish your manuscript too. If you or your colleagues have any manuscript ready for publication or are working on it, kindly contact us with detailed synopsis and list of contents. We will transform your work into a valuable publication. If you wish, we can also suggest you the suitable subjects for writing the books related to your area of expertise. Manas is known for its publishing quality and commitments. We take utmost care in production and give wide publicity to the book as well as its author through our national and international distribution network.

KASHMIR IS FREE

A novel by

Arun Kumar, IAS (Retd)
(Jammu & Kashmir Cadre)
Prasenjeet Kumar

Manas Publications
(We Convert Fighters into Writers)
New Delhi - 110 002 (INDIA)

MANAS PUBLICATIONS
(We Convert Fighters into Writers)
(Publishers, Library Suppliers, Importers & Exporters)
4402/5-A, Ansari Road (Opp. HDFC Bank)
Darya Ganj, New Delhi - 110 002 (India)
Phones: Off.: 011-23260783, 23265523, Res.: 011-23842660
E-mail: manaspublications@gmail.com
manaspublications@yahoo.com
Website: www.manaspublications.in

ISBN 978-81-7049-552-9
₹ 795

Designed by
Veronica Grafic Arts

Printed in India at
R.K. Print Services, Delhi
and published by Mrs Suman Lata for
Manas Publications
4402/5-A, Ansari Road (Opp HDFC Bank)
Darya Ganj, New Delhi - 110 002 (INDIA)

To

All My Friends

who think the plot of this book can

NEVER *come true.*

May they all be proved correct.

Destiny has two ways of crushing us – by refusing our wishes and by fulfilling them.

– Henri-Frédéric Amiel

Prologue
Srinagar, 29 March 2022

SHABIR Ahmad Kaloo, editor of *The Kashmir Front*, stroked his trim Kashmiri beard as he punched furiously on his laptop. Then with a flourish, he finished his piece: "The PM of India, Are You Listening?"

As he slouched back in his swivelling office chair, Shabir gave his editorial a final once over.

Looks all right … enough to give the Indian agencies another sleepless night, he smirked as he scratched his sharp aquiline nose.

A whiff of air from the open window suddenly blew away some paper from Shabir's desk, which was, in any case, cluttered with all kinds of reports, newspaper clippings, and files. Instinctively, Shabir bent down to pick those up from the floor. And winced in pain.

"Bloody hell!" he whimpered, as his fingers also picked up some dirt from the unswept floor.

Looks like the sweeper has not been coming for quite some time, thanks to the frequent hartals in the city.

Surrounded as it was by all kinds of buildings, Shabir's office in downtown Srinagar had no natural light. And the musty smell was now all-pervading. That's why the windows had to be kept open.

Just then, he heard a knock on his door.

"Come in," he said.

A tall lanky clean shaven Kashmiri man entered his room.

Shabir looked up. "Ah Khurshid! There you are."

Khurshid entered the room with a laptop bag. He took a seat facing the editor.

"Did you manage to get what I'd asked for?"

"Yes, Sir," Khurshid said hesitantly. He opened his laptop and showed the pictures to Shabir.

"I think this one would be appropriate."

Shabir adjusted his round spectacles that gave him, as he was told, a decidedly intellectual look, and stared intently at the picture of a dead young girl. Her head covered in a scarf, scars all over her face and her eyes closed. Her face – so peaceful.

"Perfect. Is it from the *paar* folder?" Shabir asked referring to the stock images sent by the Pakistani agencies from across the border.

"Yes Sir. So, if we use this image, we will get paid extra. But Sir … just to clarify, this girl is not Kashmiri. She's probably a Syrian who was killed in an US air strike conducted against the ISIS."

"Doesn't matter," Shabir replied, "The girl looks Kashmiri, and the image fits the editorial I've just finished…. So just email the picture to production and you can leave."

Shabir proof read his editorial once again giving it some final touches. The production then uploaded the article along with the photo of the girl as a front-page editorial.

The editorial's last few paras read:

> "For how long, will you keep on killing us? For how long? Just yesterday, your Indian Army gang-raped and mercilessly killed a 16-year-old innocent Kashmiri girl. Her only fault – she was good looking. And, of course, that – she was a Kashmiri.
>
> Mr Indian PM, do you know why young men are pelting stones at your army? Want to know the real reason? The reason is, that we're sick and tired of your farce democrazy, your manipulated elections, your governments imposed from Delhi, a democracy that has no place in the world we are trying to build in Kashmir.
>
> You've exploited us since 1947. You have bartered our water and exploited mercilessly our power and mineral resources. And when we raise our voice, you kill our boys and rape our women. Someday, Insha'Allah, you'll have to pay for this all.
>
> It's no longer the fringe, Mr Indian PM. Every boy and girl on the street is throwing stones at you, and at all your instruments of coercion, loot, and plunder. It's a revolution. A mass movement. How many will you kill, Mr Indian PM?
>
> You have no option but to leave and give us our cherished azaadi."

As Shabir swivelled back in satisfaction, he experienced another sharp pain on the left side of his abdomen. He winced as he massaged that side of his belly. The pain now radiated to his back. His breathing became laboured.

The pain had been bothering him for quite some time. And so Shabir had consulted his school friend, Dr Anil Koul, a nephrologist with Apollo Hospitals, who advised him to rush immediately to Delhi for some advanced tests for his kidneys. Shabir could have scheduled an appointment in Srinagar in SKIMS (Sher-i-Kashmir Institute of Medical Sciences), but he had no faith in the local doctors. Most were so busy minting money that they had little time to keep up with the latest developments in their respective medical disciplines.

Funny Anil Koul, Shabir mused, thinking about his friend who was the declared *joker* of their class because he was always joking! His family too had 'migrated' out of the Valley in those turbulent 1990s because of the threats from those Islamist zealots, as they claimed. But Shabir's belief was that it was that evil Governor Jagmohan who had asked the Kashmiri Pandits to 'run away' so that he could have a freer hand crushing the Muslims. Shabir and Anil could never agree on what was the real cause but had remained friends regardless.

His mobile buzzed. It was Air India.

"Mr Kaloo, Shabir Ahmad Kaloo?"

As Shabir confirmed, the chirpy female voice on the other end continued, "Sir, we apologise, but your flight for April 1, 2022 on Air India AI 0825 for the Srinagar-Delhi sector has been cancelled for technical reasons."

Bloody hell! Bloody Air India?!

"Okay, but would you be then making any substitute arrangements?" Shabir asked sharply.

There was silence for a few seconds.

"I'm sorry Sir," announced the female voice on the other end, "but all our flights are running full. Your payment is being refunded and will be credited within 24 hours to the credit card you used for the booking."

There was a sudden rude click at the other end disconnecting the call.

That was no help. *But what the hell? What else did you expect from this perpetually bankrupt national carrier?*

So Shabir logged on to his favourite MakeMyTrip site and looked for flights for 1 April. Usually, there were some twenty non-stop flights from Srinagar to Delhi every day. So, he was confident he would be able to find another flight. But funnily, all flights looked fully booked.

Desperate, he tried yatra.com, goibibo.com, cleartrip.com, and then the websites of Jet Airways, IndiGo, GoAir, Vistara, SpiceJet, AirAsia – every airline site he could recall. No seats still. He tried via Jammu, via Chandigarh, even via Leh, and then looked for 2nd, 3rd, and 4th April, but the result was infuriatingly the same.

This was crazy. The tourist season was a month away, and still the flights were all packed.

Unbelievable!

One option was to go to the Srinagar Airport that day and try finding a seat on any airline that was flying out. But in the security-crazy airport area that wasn't so easy. You had to have a valid ticket before you could enter the area. But how can you have a valid ticket if the airlines were not offering any?

The only way to short-circuit the security, Shabir knew, was to declare you were going to receive someone. But for that too, you needed an official vehicle. Or an authorised travel agent who could give you a lift.

Anyway. These were the only two options Shabir could think of, and so, after a few calls, the influential editor of the *Kashmir Front* managed to locate the driver of an IAS officer who was going to the airport on that day to pickup his boss.

* * *

Came the D-day, and surprisingly Shabir could make it to the arrival area of the Srinagar Airport with no hiccups. The glass building with its sharply sloping roofs was designed to look like snow covered Himalayas. But to Shabir, the airport looked more like a bunker. A reminder of India's colonisation of Kashmir.

He thanked the driver profusely and rang up his contact in the security who escorted him to the airline ticket counters OUTSIDE the terminal building.

"This is the maximum I can do Shabir Saheb," the police man told him. "You have to have a ticket now for entering the departure area."

Fortunately, there were no queues at the counters. But that was a no brainer.

There were no queues because there were still no vacant seats on any airline.

Meanwhile, flights circled overhead and kept on landing. Passengers kept on arriving in droves on all kinds of vehicles and kept on getting inside the building.

It was almost after half-an-hour of waiting that Shabir could observe an interesting phenomenon. The passengers flying out all appeared to be non-Kashmiris. Most were in uniform, from the army or BSF, CRPF, or any of the other tens of para-military outfits posted in the Valley.

But strangely, all the flights that were landing in were only disgorging Kashmiris – men, women, children, all looking quite flustered. *There were no Indian or foreign tourists at all.*

After observing for an hour, Shabir couldn't control himself and approached an arriving family – seemed like husband, wife, son, and daughter.

"*Bhai Saheb*, is everything all right," he asked.

The man and his wife and children exchanged glances.

"How the hell do we know?" the man exploded.

Shabir slunk back, shocked, and speechless.

Fifteen minutes later, he approached a departing man in uniform, "Sirji, are you flying out today?"

"Obviously I am. But why are you asking? Aren't you a Kashmiri?"

"Yes, why?"

"Then you should be happy you've got what you've been asking for," he said. And then looking at Shabir's quizzical face added, "your blasted *Azaadi*, what else? So, enjoy your freedom now. And don't bother to come to India. Ever."

Year 2020

1

Shopian, 1 January 2020

THE army convoy was passing through the sleepy town of Shopian in Kashmir when a mob charged in and isolated a truck. The crowd began building up as it surrounded the truck from all sides.

Hundreds of people marched towards the vehicle. Mostly in their late teens or early twenties. Wearing a green band around their heads. Their faces covered. They chanted slogans. *Hum kya chahe? Azaadi. Azaadi ka matlab kya? La-illahah ill-lallah. Naray-e-taqbir-allahu-akbar.* What we want is freedom. Freedom meaning the rule of Allah. Long live the revolution. God is great.

The crowd began throwing stones which hit the truck like little missiles.

Major Uday Varman's blood pressure was rising as he watched the scene unfold. His colleague Captain Ismail Multani also of the 10th Garhwal Rifles took out his mobile phone and began recording the incident. Wireless sets were crackling in every truck with soldiers seeking permission to disembark and come to the rescue of the stranded truck.

"No," Major Verman kept on repeating, "How will you fight this crowd? We have no batons or shield or any riot-police gear."

"Sir, permission to fire in the air then?" Captain Multani requested.

"Granted."

One soldier moved forwards and fired in the air. Some startled pigeons flew out from the tinned rooftops. But the crowd hesitated only for a moment as they figured out where the shot was aimed at. Then again, they kept moving closer to the truck.

"Fire another round," Major Verman ordered.

Another shot was fired in the air. But the mob kept pelting stones. A stone hit a soldier's jaw and he let out a shriek and tumbled backwards. Blood dripped from his jaw as he spat out a broken tooth. Another stone hit a soldier's left eye. Nothing much remained of that eye. Just blood and a big round black scar.

The crowd was now putting logs and twigs under the truck to set it on fire.

"The crowd is relentless. Sir, we can't wait," Ismail implored.

Major Varman closed his eyes for a second. He hated doing this. But they were running out of options.

"Yes Captain, enough is enough. I cannot let any more of my boys get injured. Fire, but aim at the lower portions, if possible."

"Yes, Sir."

As the soldiers opened fire at the crowd, the mob ran in the opposite direction creating a stampede. People screamed and shouted. The streets deserted soon leaving behind mounds of stones and slippers. The news reported two dead in the incident – identified as a 20-year-old Naveed Ahmad Bhat and 24-year-old Ibrahim Ghani Lone. Twenty were injured, some critically.

*   *   *

CM Hasina Ittoo sat in her office watching the TV where a hyper-ventilating Kashmiri anchor was narrating how the Indian Army had gone berserk in Shopian. A woman in her mid-50s, she had covered her head in a scarf in the classic Islamic style, even when she was indoors. The Director General of Police (DGP) Suresh Goyal stood in front of her.

"DGP Saheb, what's this all?" Anger clearly in her tone.

"Yes Madam ... two people are dead as per the latest report," said Suresh sheepishly, as if it was all his fault.

"What? How dare they kill our *children*? Are *they* running the government or we are?"

"The army says they fired in self-defence. Otherwise they'd have all been lynched and burnt."

"That's nonsense," CM Ittoo screamed. "They fired indiscriminately at so many people. They're bloody murderers. How can we sit watching so many innocent Kashmiris losing their lives like this?"

"Madam," Suresh said. "The crowd was throwing stones at the convoy –"

"So that justifies the use of bullets? Huh? Is that what you're saying? Bullets for stones. Since when we have started firing on peaceful protesters? *Do logon ki jaane chali gayi aur aap mujhe yeh safaayi de rahein hain."* Two people have lost their lives, and this is the explanation you come up with?

CM Ittoo pushed the files aside on her table and swivelled in her chair. There was dead silence in the room. She then turned towards Suresh. "So, what's next?"

"Madam, we've arrested a few culprits who were throwing stones at the convoy."

"What? How dare you?" CM Ittoo pounded her fist on the table. "Suresh, how many times have I told you to show restraint? They're just children who have misbehaved somewhat. RELEASE THEM NOW. And ..." She paused. "One more thing. File a FIR (First Information Report) against the army. And that Major ... What's his name?"

"Major Uday Varman," Suresh said not liking the whole thing even one bit.

CM Ittoo shook her head in a typical Kashmiri way. "Yes, that fellow. Book him for murder and attempt to murder ... and whatever sections you can think of. Throw the whole book at him."

Suresh's jaw remained open. "Madam, this has never been done before."

"DGP Saheb," CM Ittoo said firmly. *"Agar aap kam nahin kar sakte hain, toh bata deejiye."* (If you cannot do the work, then let me know.)

Suresh closed his eyes and took a deep breath. "Your orders will be carried out, Madam."

* * *

Lt Col (retired) Karan Varman, Major Uday Varman's father, moved the Supreme Court with a petition to quash the FIR. *My son did nothing wrong. The mob was violent. Two of his colleagues were injured critically. Had he not ordered the firing, they would have all been lynched. Just as DSP Mohammad Ayub Pandith was lynched on June 23, 2017 outside a Srinagar mosque.*

The petition also claimed that the FIR would demoralise the armed forces.

The Supreme Court directed the Jammu & Kashmir Government to explain why the FIR registered against the army should not be quashed. The case is yet to be decided.

* * *

The FIR was a big news nationally. Journalists lined outside CM Ittoo's office to get her 'sound bite'. When she came out, the reporters surrounded her pushing one mike after the other.

"Madam," one reporter said. "Major Uday Varman's father has filed a petition in the Supreme Court. He says the FIR would demoralise the army. What do you have to say?"

Adjusting her huge dark glasses, CM Ittoo shook her head, and tried to look sad. "A single FIR cannot demoralise our great army ... I don't buy this. Army is an institution which on the whole has done a great job defending us from external aggressors. But there can be a few black sheep anywhere, in any institution, big or small, good or bad ... who exceed their brief, and it is our duty to identify and punish them."

With that, CM Ittoo got inside her car and shut the door. The car moved and picked up speed leaving everyone behind.

2

New Delhi, 1 January 2020

PRIME Minister Chiman Bhai Patel grimaced as he switched off the TV after watching J&K CM giving her 'bite' at the FIR issue. *This lady is so fickle.*

Last time when she was pulled up by the Government of India for defending some stone-pelters who were hurt by pellet guns, she had turned around and asked in her press conference. *"Bachche wahan kya karne gaye the? Koi doodh thode na khareed rahe the?"* What were the children doing there (in the mob when they got hurt in police action)? They hadn't gone there to buy milk for sure?

But at the same time, she had implemented a policy whereby the family members of slain Islamist terrorists were awarded compensation by the Government of India. Her logic: When soldiers die, their families are given compensation. Why shouldn't the same logic apply to terrorists? After all, their family members weren't at fault. Then why should they be punished?

There is no option but to go ahead with the Operation.

He returned to the open file of 'shortlisted officers' that he was going through before the TV had distracted him. Chiman Bhai was in his second five-year term as the Prime Minister of India and his party – Bharatiya Independent Party or the BIP – ruled in almost twenty-five out of twenty-nine States. His white beard and round frameless glasses gave him a Zen master like appearance, which his detractors considered phony, but which his followers adored.

When his eyes got tired, he took a moment to admire the geometric designs of the red carpet, the wood-panelled walls, the 150-year-old chandelier and the colonial arches of his classy office that were so reminiscent of British India.

Prime Minister Chiman Bhai Patel had always been in the news for all the wrong reasons, and right reasons. He was known for ramming through 'unpopular' decisions if *he* thought they were right for the country. And the opposition was always at his throat. He had been called names ranging from Hitler to a mass murderer to a psychopath to even impotent! But the poor and the downtrodden of the country apparently couldn't care less and so, he was voted to power for the second time with a thumping majority.

Now he was working on a special mission – the mission which he didn't have the mandate to push through in his first term. The mission which would free ₹ 1,00,000 crore of India's tax payers' money. For India's development.

He glanced through the CV of Major General GS Sandhu. Recommended by the Army Chief for the post of GOC (General Officer Commanding) 15 Corps, Srinagar. As a young officer, General Sandhu had served in 1999 in the Kargil War. Internationally, he had headed the UN peace-keeping missions in Somalia, Yemen, Croatia, and Iraq. In Jammu & Kashmir, he had served all the three regions –

Ladakh, Kashmir, and Jammu. On top of that, he had spent a decade successfully leading many counter-terror operations in the Kashmir Valley. So, he was both battle hardened and well versed with the Jihadi mindset.

The IB (Intelligence Bureau) report in its 'pen picture' had concluded, "General Sandhu is a sensitive officer who knows how to balance his fierce sense of nationalism, with the exigencies on the ground. He is also one of those rare military officers who has no problem co-ordinating with his civilian counterparts in executing any task that is assigned to him."

PM Patel flicked through the pages of the biodata of the other two shortlisted army officers. To him, they all looked competent, but yes, General Sandhu did appear to have served for almost 10 years in J&K. So, no doubt, he was the most experienced for any J&K operation.

The PM's eyes lingered a little more on the colour photograph of General Sandhu. As a fiercely proud Sikh stared back at him, the PM closed his eyes and contemplated for a moment. His gut feeling was that he could count on this officer to deliver what he wanted. Exactly.

The PM's reverie was broken as he heard a knock on the door. The orderly ushered in Sanjeev Choudhary, the Cabinet Secretary. Sanjeev was nearly six feet tall and six feet wide, as his colleagues joked. Even a little movement could make him huff and puff. And sweat profusely, even in Delhi winters. Covering a distance from the door to the PM's desk was like moving from Kashmir to Kanyakumari that is from one end of India to the other.

"Come in Sanjeev. Have a seat."

Sanjeev grabbed one and sat down gasping for breath. He took out a handkerchief and wiped his forehead.

"Some water?" The PM pushed a glass of water towards him.

"Oh! Thank you, Sir." Sanjeev gulped down the whole glass in one go. He placed the glass on the table and exhaled deeply.

"Okay," the PM said, "I've seen the list for GOC 15 Corps. Who is next?"

The CabSec (Cabinet Secretary) turned the pages, "Sir, we next have the list of officers who will be handling the Air Force, CRPF, BSF, ITBP, SSB, IB, and R&AW operations...."

"No," the PM held up his hand to stop the barrage of information which could have sure overloaded his systems.

"I'd leave these decisions to their respective heads. But I'd like to focus on two positions – the Governor, and the Chief Secretary. Do we have a short-list ready?"

"Sir, for the Governor," Sanjeev explained, "I have had a small discussion with the Honourable Home Minister. And we have made a panel of three names for your consideration."

"And who are they?"

"Sir, first is an army officer. In fact, we're recommending the current Army Chief General Hussain. He's retiring next year. General Hussain is a thorough professional. Like General Sandhu, he knows J&K like the back of his hand. He's an Indian first, and a Muslim later. But ... as a Muslim, he could be more acceptable in the Valley which is now, as we know, 99.9% Muslim."

"No!" the PM's voice was uncharacteristically sharp. "This is not exactly an army operation. Governor J&K is also the statutory head of Shri Mata Vaishno Devi and Amarnathji Shrine Boards. For a Muslim, it could be a little dicey. I'd rather prefer a Hindu and a civilian for this project."

"In that case, Sir, we're suggesting Shri MS Balasubramanian. Lawyer, social activist, politician, Harvard professor, and even an ex-CM of Tamil Nadu. He's very knowledgeable on matters concerning J&K. He's also an authority on Islam and Islamic terrorism. I think you know him very well, Sir."

"Yes," the PM nodded. "I know Bala very well. He's brilliant no doubt. But he's also an *unguided missile*. If we send him to J&K, he'll be bound to pursue his own agenda. Sooner than later. And then who'll rein him in?"

"You have a point, Sir. In that case may I suggest some retired IAS officer?" And Sanjeev proceeded to pull out three more CVs.

The PM flicked through the pages but was not focused. His mind wandered. Just the previous night he had finished reading a brilliant memoir of an IAS officer of J&K cadre.

"Sanjeev?"

"Yes Sir?"

"Have you read that book? What is it called ... er ... *The Outsider's Curse?*"

"Oh, yes Sir, I have ... as most IAS officers would have. The book focuses on the problems that AIS (All-India Service) officers go through while serving J&K. Like they can't buy property, educate their children in medical or engineering colleges, vote in elections –"

"No," interrupted the PM, "I don't want your views about those deprivations, which are all there, no doubt. What I wanted to know is ... what do you think of this officer who has written that book?"

"Monali Kumar?!" Sanjeev's jaw remained open in surprise, bordering on horror.

The PM frowned. "What's the matter?"

"Sir," Sanjeev answered. "I know Madam Monali Kumar very well. She was three years senior to me. And we used to meet regularly during the informal lunch club ... in Shastri

Bhavan … when we were both in the HRD (Human Resource Development) Ministry." Sanjeev looked up at the white ceiling trying to figure when he had met her last. "In the early 1990s I think."

PM Patel was quiet as he stared at Sanjeev with his Zen looks. The silence in the room was deafening. PM sensed that Sanjeev was speaking a lot without saying much. Sanjeev looked here and there not knowing what to say next.

"So?" the PM asked.

"Monaliji was very popular. Friendly with everyone – from the lowly peons to the high-flying Secretaries. But …" Sanjeev stopped as his eyes widened. "Sir, you are NOT considering her for the post of Governor J&K, are you?"

"Why? Do you have any objections?"

"No, Sir," Sanjeev clarified. His tone indicated otherwise. That was the great thing about Sanjeev – his uncanny ability to fathom what his bosses wanted and to deliver that – exactly. That's why, regimes came and went but Sanjeev remained the darling of every one. Graduating from being the Private Secretary to insignificant Ministers of State, to Private Secretary of powerful Cabinet Ministers, to Principal Secretary to corrupt and whimsical Chief Ministers, to Secretary to hide-bound Governors, and now he was the all-powerful Cabinet Secretary.

"Integrity wise," Sanjeev was continuing, "no one can lift a little finger at her. Nationalist, she's hard-core. Kashmir, being a J&K cadre officer, she knows very well. The problem is – she knows J&K just too well. That's why, we generally send Governors who are complete outsiders to that State. But in case of Madam Monali…."

"She's an insider, despite being an outsider," the PM exclaimed. "I quite like that."

"But … Sir, there is a problem."

The PM frowned. "And what is that?"

"Sir …" Sanjeev took a long pause. "She's very opinionated…." He was looking for a more appropriate diplomatic word to describe her, but this was all he could come up with.

"She has a mind of her own. And when she takes a decision, she doesn't back down. When she was serving J&K, she took some so-called unpopular decisions that didn't go down well with the then J&K Government. May I suggest –"

"No, don't bother, because that's exactly the kind of officer I need," the PM interrupted. "By the way, where is this officer nowadays?"

"Sir, to the best of my knowledge, she has after retirement settled down in Greater Noida, in a colony of government officers. She was contacted for some post-retirement sinecures, but she flatly refused. She said she didn't want to be a *ghulam* (slave) any more. Her passion nowadays, I'm told, is writing short-stories on Kashmir on the *Outsider* theme. And looking after the affairs of the small co-operative housing society she stays in."

"I'd like to meet her," the PM desired. "Could you please organise that?"

"Sure Sir." Hesitation in Sanjeev's tone.

"That'll be all for today. Let's meet Monaliji first."

Sanjeev got up. He tried to bow but his paunch came in the way. Still, he bowed slightly and uncomfortably, and left.

3

Greater Noida, 4 January 2020

IT was a bitterly cold Saturday morning. There were hardly any morning walkers in the community park of Sector Omega-I of Greater Noida. The few who were there, were startled by a loud roaring sound. The sound of a chopper flying too low. Or something like that.

A huge Mi-17 helicopter of the Indian Air Force with a bull's eye painted on both its sides broke out of the slightly overcast skies and swooped down on the sports ground adjoining the community park. But instead of landing, it just touched the ground and took off again.

The sight scared the walkers who scattered in different directions, bewildered.

"Ground sanitised.... Landing cleared," the pilot shouted.

"Roger, Victor Charlie 213, landing in two minutes," the pilot of the other Mi-17 replied.

In no time, another Mi-17 appeared over the sports ground. Soon it was hovering twenty feet above the playground and then it slowly descended and made contact with the brown grassless ground.

As commandos in black dress pushed the UP policemen back to secure the helicopter, the rotors stopped. A door opened and a step-down ladder was placed out.

Four persons got down and immediately got into two gleaming black 7-series BMWs. Another BMW escorted these vehicles in the front and yet another followed them in the rear. Once outside the sports ground, an UP Police Toyota Innova escorted the motorcade to its destination. A government ambulance waiting on the roadside brought up the rear.

* * *

Monali Kumar had just returned from her morning walk and was taking off her walking shoes. She checked the Fitbit watch on her wrist and was pleased to find that she had just reached her goal of 10,000 steps. As usual. *Fantastic!* A smile creased her lips as she quietly congratulated herself. There had not been even a single day when she couldn't complete her task of walking at least 10,000 steps. Most of the time, it actually hovered around 20,000.

That was when she heard some vehicles driving in and screeching to a stop. Which broke her reverie. *What the hell was that?!*

Curious, she peeped out of her bay window. And saw the incongruous sight of – as many as four bulletproof BMWs – stopping right in front of her house. Two policemen had already alighted from a Toyota Innova and were running to open the gate – the gate to her house.

What do these guys want?! Monali thought as the doorbell rang.

As she opened the main door of her house, she gasped. It was the PM's motorcade. The same motorcade composed of those gleaming $1.5 million BMW 7-series 760Li which she had seen so many times in J&K. The cars were reportedly bulletproofed in the BMW factory itself in Germany and could withstand AK-47 attacks which the J&K bulletproofed vehicles couldn't.

And there was Shri Chiman Bhai Patel, the PM, in flesh, getting out of the second BMW and heading straight to her house. As usual, the PM was dressed well in a starched Jodhpur *bandgulla* suit.

And was that tall bald man, Mr Sapru, the Home Minister, on his right? And who was that fat man barely able to walk? Sanjeev, the Cabinet Secretary?

"Monaliji, *Namaskar*. Sorry to disturb you so early in the morning. But can you spare us five-minutes?" the PM asked.

"S-Sir. D-Do come in, please. What a pleasant surprise, and a great honour this is. I hope everything is all right. But why did you bother, Sir? You could have asked me to come over."

The PM sighed. "I tried, Monaliji, but your phone was switched off, I was told." The PM looked at Sanjeev.

"I think it is still switched off, Sir. As it usually is from 10 PM to 10 AM. Isn't it Madam?" Sanjeev said, with a mischievous smile creasing his lips.

"Oh, come on Sanjeev," Monali protested as she ushered them to her drawing room. "There could be a hundred other ways to reach me."

"Madam, I sent you a text message too. But that was after 10 PM yesterday, I suppose. So, you'll see that whenever you switch on your mobile today. I then sent you a message through your colony's security guards."

Monali put a hand on her mouth to stop the exclamation of horror that was about to escape her lips. She remembered the guard who had come to her house last night with a message that the PM wanted to talk to her on such-and-such number. That the message had come from some Cabinet Secretary. And she had thought that was a prank and asked him to buzz off!

"Any way, Monaliji, forget all that," the PM interrupted. "We are here about a mission that couldn't wait."

Monali was speechless.

"But first, let me commend you on your book – *The Outsider's Curse* … that I finished yesterday. The book has opened my eyes about the happenings in J&K … which, to be frank, I had very little clue about." The PM then turned towards Sapru. "Sapruji, you should also read that book when you've some time."

"Thank you, Sir. Thank you for your kind words," Monali could only muster this much.

Just then, Bagheera, the old Ladakhi mongrel, sauntered in to investigate and started sniffing everyone's shoes.

"I hope he doesn't bite," a wary Sapru remarked.

"No Sir," Monali smiled. "Ladakhis only bite Kashmiris, not Indians."

Every one guffawed.

"So Sapru Saheb, you have to decide whether you're an Indian or a Kashmiri," the PM chuckled. He then turned towards Monali.

"Monaliji, the mission we're bothering you is connected to the theme of your memoir. That insider-outsider problem. That we'd like to sort out for once. And for all. With your help, of course."

"My help? I don't understand. What exactly do you want from me, Sir?"

The Prime Minister was silent for a moment as he stared at the ceiling. Then he dropped the bombshell. "I want you to go to J&K to help carry out a very important task."

"Go to J&K?!" Alarm clearly in Monali's voice. "And do that dreaded 6-monthly *Durbar Move* again? That I have ranted so much against in my memoir?" She paused. "No, Sir, thank you so much."

"Monaliji?! Let me complete my offer," the PM sighed. "I want you to go to J&K ... in national interest ... as Governor to help carry out a very important *Operation* that we're working on. And who said anything about *Durbar Move*?"

Monali was stumped for a moment. "The Governor of J&K?"

"Monaliji, I have to rush back. So, what I'll do is leave Sanjeev behind ... who'll explain everything about this *Operation* ... where after I hope you will agree to spearhead that mission in national interest. Thank you so much for seeing us at this unearthly hour." The PM got up and folded his hands.

Monali also got up and folded her hands.

"Come on Sapruji, let's move. *Namaskar Monaliji, phir milenge*. See you soon."

As Monali saw the PM and the Home Minister off, the BMWs roared to life and the motorcade sped to the sports ground. Within minutes, the Mi-17s were up in the air and flying towards Delhi to the Safdarjung Airport.

4

Cabinet Meeting, New Delhi, 8 January 2020

DEFENCE Minister Naidu was snoring in his bed when the villain woke him up with a start. Yes, the villain – the RAX (Rural Automatic Exchange, as it was originally called) placed on the bedside table ringing incessantly. The digital clock on that secure intercom instrument showed 0145 hrs.

Has war broken out somewhere? Naidu wondered, as he lifted the hand set and said, "Haloooo...."

"Sorry to bother you, Sir. This is TSR from the PMO (Prime Minister's Office)."

There was no mistaking the voice of TS Ramakrishnan, the trusted aide of the PM from the Gujarat cadre of the IAS.

"Yes, Ramki, what's it?" Naidu was now fully awake.

"Sir, the Honourable PM wants to see you at 0230 hrs. Now," TSR said without offering even a hint of an apology.

"*Okkay*, I'll be there," Naidu replied in his thick Telugu accent and got up to wear something more decent.

At 0225 hrs, Naidu had reached 1, Race Course Road, sorry the Lok Kalyan Road, the official residence of the Prime Minister of India. There appeared to be a mini traffic jam ahead.

At this godforsaken hour? Naidu shook his head in disbelief.

Then he realised that all those vehicles were turning towards the PM's residence. Once inside the gates, and after they had gone through the full-body scanner, the vehicles started stopping at the reception. The first to alight was Mr Sapru, the Home Minister. With him was Mr Daniel, the National Security Adviser (NSA). Next was Mr Birla, the Finance Minister. Naidu was the third Cabinet Minister to alight.

After a cursory walk through the door-frame metal detector, where polite security staff collected his mobile, Naidu was ushered into the PM's Conference Room. He was still half asleep and walked like a moving corpse.

The room was almost half full. The three service chiefs – of the Army, Air Force, and Navy were already there. The Director Generals (DGs) of the BSF (Border Security Force), CRPF (Central Reserve Police Force), CISF (Central Industrial Security Force), and ITBP (Indo-Tibetan Border Police) were also in attendance. The Cabinet Secretary, Foreign Secretary, Defence Secretary, Finance Secretary, and the Home Secretary had already taken their seats.

Naidu nodded at the senior officers and his cabinet colleagues and moved to take the seat on the right-hand side of the Prime Minister where his name plate was placed. He was rubbing his eyes that were still red from a lack of sleep.

Exactly at 0231 hrs, the PM entered the room. As everyone got up to greet, the PM motioned them to sit down.

Switching off the mike in front of his seat, as his booming voice needed no boost, the PM addressed the gathering.

"Friends, I'm sorry to have dragged you out so early on a winter morning. But this couldn't wait.... It's time we launched *Operation Load shedding.*"

There was pin-drop silence in the room, but the shock at the faces of the participants was telling.

"The decision was made last year, as you all know. But the timing of the launch was to be firmed up. And we have decided that to be 1 April 2022 – about two years or rather twenty-six months from now. So, let the countdown begin," the PM said. The lack of emotion in his voice was startling.

"Today will be the last and final opportunity to discuss all implications," the PM continued, "So, please feel free to voice your doubts, apprehensions, misgivings, objections...."

"There are some new faces today who were not there when we had first discussed this *Operation* last year. So, let me start with them first."

The PM turned towards General Hussain. "General Saheb, have you acquainted yourself with the operational details of what I'm talking about?"

"Yes Sir," General Hussain answered. As the first Muslim Chief in the history of independent India, Hussain knew how careful he had to be in his handling of this *ultra-sensitive* matter.

"Very well," the PM nodded. "Let's then understand the *Operation* from the army's point of view."

"Sir, as I understand, Indian Army's brief is to retreat with minimum casualties and disruption –"

"No!" the PM interrupted. General Hussain paused and wondered what he'd said wrong.

"Not with minimum casualties, General," the PM said. "But with NIL casualties."

"Right Sir, nil casualties." General Hussain quickly regained his composure. "May I now present the full case?"

As the PM nodded, General Hussain used the remote to switch on the main 65-inch TV screen, flanked with one 50-inch screen each on either side of the round table.

As one PowerPoint slide followed another, the gathering watched intently. The slides started with the D-day and followed backwards to D-day minus 900 days. So, the army wanted almost three years to complete the *Operation*.

As the PM looked quizzically at the General, the Chief entered 1 April 2022 as the D-day on his tablet, and the software adjusted all completion dates accordingly. Formation by formation, base by base, the steps were outlined in excruciating detail.

"Good," the PM nodded. "Any questions?"

As he looked around, a hand went up. It was Mr Birla, the Finance Minister.

"General Saheb, I just wanted to know the financial implications of the entire exercise. Will we save money? Which is more or less the objective for this entire *Operation*, isn't it? Or will we be out-of-pocket somewhat? Because then I've to provide for that deficit in the budget."

"Good point, Birla Saheb," the PM nodded and invited the General to explain.

"Sir, our current strength in the Kashmir Valley hovers around 1,00,000 boots on the ground. Transporting them in the three-month period from 1 January to 31 March 2022 will be a logistical nightmare. But in financial terms, the *Operation* will be a bonanza. As we'll no longer be transporting supplies for so many soldiers so far away from our stores in the plains."

"We also don't own any land in the Valley. But instead pay a lease rent to the State Government to the tune of ₹40 crore annually. That will be an immediate saving, I suppose."

"Where we'll lose out will be the structures we leave behind. You know, the residential quarters, messes, auditoriums, golf courses, exercise tracks, field artillery ranges, and so on. If we could be compensated somewhat for those facilities…."

"That has been taken care of," the Finance Minister explained. "We have to compute the present value of all these facilities and compensate the army by appropriating the J&K Government properties elsewhere in the country."

"That will be great, Sir." General Hussain said and disconnected the Bluetooth on his tablet.

The screen turned blank for a moment. Immediately, the approved Government of India screen-saver of the Indian flag fluttering in the wind started playing on the monitors.

"Should we have the Air Force next?" The PM looked at Air Chief Marshal Pintoo Masani, who started setting up his presentation.

Just then, the PM sensed something and turned to General Hussain. "General Saheb, is there something else bothering you?"

"Actually … yes, Sir." General Hussain sounded hesitant.

"And … what is it?"

"Sir, we're here to carry out your orders, regardless of the costs and hardships. We also know how firm you're in your convictions."

The PM nodded but said nothing.

"I was thinking … even if there be a 1% chance of the army ever being sent back to the Valley, after the D-day, we'll be in a serious mess."

"Tell me more, General Saheb."

"Once we abandon our bunkers and all our defensive positions, it'll be virtually impossible to capture them back."

The PM said nothing.

"We'll then be monitoring the situation through our drones and satellites, from the skies, just as the Americans do in Afghanistan. The implications of putting back any soldiers on the ground will be horrendous to even contemplate."

"Thank you, General Saheb." The PM didn't bother to answer any of the General's doubts. He then turned towards the Air Chief. "Chief Masani, are you ready?"

"Yes Sir," Masani answered and clicked on his tablet to start his presentation.

5

Srinagar, 8 January 2020

THE Court of the Financial Commissioner (Revenue) or FC(R), had just been called to order. Raj Verma, the FC(R), was in the 'chair', which was placed in front of a massive table. That was flanked on both sides by two chairs each accommodating the three readers, and Raj's Personal Secretary. The whole setup was put on a platform about two feet higher than the rest of the wood-panelled courtroom keeping in with the majesty of this highest revenue court of J&K.

Raj experienced butterflies in his stomach. He had never been a judge before and didn't know what he was expected to do. Although he was a Punjabi, in J&K, he was more or less considered a *Madrasi* as he was somewhat dark complexioned. He had reached the highest pay grade of his service, of a Financial Commissioner in the State Government, which was equal to a Secretary in the Government of India. Age-wise, he was in his mid-50s but looked much younger as if he were in his early 40s. He adjusted his spectacles and prepared himself for the hearing.

"Ahmed Bhat *vs* Nazir Gojri," the Reader, a revenue official in the rank of Naib-Tehsildar, shouted. He was called the *Reader* because his main job was to *read* the revenue records which were all maintained in Urdu, in Persian script, in such bad handwriting that only an experienced *reader* could make any sense out of them!

Everyone looked here and there, but no one approached the bench.

"Next," Raj Verma nodded.

"Manjoor Kumar *vs* Mehjoor Kumar," the Reader announced.

"Present Sir," said Haji Abdul Raouf, the veteran revenue lawyer, a thin gawky man with a flowing white beard and moustache, as he moved to the left of the bench. He was called *Haji* because he had *successfully* performed the Muslim holy pilgrimage of *Haj* in Saudi Arabia.

"I'm representing the defendant," announced Nazir Ahmed, the President of the Revenue Bar Association, and moved to the right. Nazir was the exact opposite of Haji. Overweight and bulky, he walked aggressively as if he were bracing up for a bull fight.

"Haji Saheb, please start," Raj said.

"Your lordship," Haji started, as Raj winced involuntarily at the archaic colonial address. "Your honour," Haji immediately corrected himself, "it's a very simple case. My father passed away in 2018, leaving behind me, his son, and three daughters."

Raj blinked for a second as he thought of commiserating with Haji Saheb for his loss. He stopped just in time as his

Reader whispered that when Haji Saheb said his father had died, he actually meant that his client's father had passed away!

What?! Raj wondered. He knew lawyers were supposed to 'represent' their clients. But in this court, the lawyers appeared to represent their clients 'literally'. His mind wandered to many legal thrillers of John Grisham and court room trials in movies he had read or watched. But nowhere could he remember lawyers referring to their clients' stories as their own. Who started this tradition in J&K then?!

"Fortunately, my father Ghaffar had left a will," Haji Saheb continued, "that desired that I, his son, be his legal *hair* ... in possession of all his property in village Kanihama measuring 30 kanals and 5 marlas. A probated copy of the will is attached with my petition requesting that my father's land be now mutated in my favour."

Raj winced at the typical Kashmiri pronunciation of *heir* as *hair*, but he let that pass and asked,

"What's the dispute then?"

"Sir, the dispute is," Nazir Ahmed the lawyer for the opposite side intervened, "that Manjoor Kumar, Haji Saheb's client, is NOT the real son of Ghaffar but an adopted son. And adoption is considered illegal under the J&K Muslim Personal Law (Shariat) Application Act, 2007."

"Your honour, I was adopted some 40 years back, by my father in 1980, which is 27 years before the Shariat Act was passed in J&K. How can you then apply a law retrospectively to my disadvantage?" Haji Saheb argued.

"Sir, as a Muslim we are all bound by Shariat, from the time of the Holy Prophet, may peace be upon him," Nazir Ahmed said, "and that forbids the pagan practice of adoption. We all know that. Therefore, Manjoor Kumar is not entitled to anything. Instead the estate has to evolve on other surviving male *hairs*, and my client being the younger brother of the deceased Ghaffar has the most legitimate claim in the matter."

"Your honour," Haji Saheb argued, "this is not fair. 40 years back, when my father adopted me, no one raised any objection in terms of Shariat or whatever. For 40 long years, I've tilled the land with my own hands and raised a lovely apple orchard with my own sweat and blood. I married off my three sisters to decent families. I looked after my father in his old age when he was ill and bed-ridden for almost two years. And finally, I made all the funeral arrangements when he left this world for his appointment with the Almighty. All this while my uncle raised no objection. Now that my father is no more, my uncle's greed recognises no human boundaries. And he has come up with this utterly vile and mischievous claim that needs to be thrown out of the window."

Raj was bewildered. Haji Saheb had a point. But only in moral terms. Now that J&K had a formal Shariat Act, there was no way he, a *Hindu judge*, could disregard that. He needed to mull things over, coolly.

"The Court is adjourned for 30 minutes," Raj announced. "We'll meet at 1230 when I shall announce my decision."

As Parvez, his burly PSO (Personal Security Officer), parted the crowds, Raj followed by his two readers and his Personal Secretary made the way to his wood-panelled office room on the first floor of the revenue complex. The view from the window, of the river Jhelum languorously winding its way through downtown Srinagar, was so much more soothing than the one from the dingy, *no-view*, court room below.

"Show me the Shariat Act please," Raj asked his senior-most reader who promptly produced the *Bare Act.*

The other reader meanwhile opened the expert commentary on the Shariat Act and was holding up the debate on adoption. There was no doubt that adoption was illegal for Muslims under the Shariat.

"Sir, this is a cut-and-dry case," the senior reader suggested. "We have no option but to rule against Haji Saheb's client."

Raj was silent. *Oh no! Not another controversy?!*

All the memories came flooding back at once. Of the infamous Amarnath controversy ... of some twelve years back in 2008. It was an election year. And all political parties and separatist leaders in Kashmir had ganged up against this annual pilgrimage to the Holy Shrine of Amarnath. The reasons they quoted were many. Pollution being the biggest. Deforestation, second. And above all, the *cultural onslaught* on the Kashmiri Muslim identity.

General Sinha (who was the Governor of J&K, and also the ex officio Chairman of the Amarnath Shrine Board) had ordered Raj (as the CEO of that Board) to hold a press conference and clarify matters.

Raj had tried to do exactly that. He remembered the press conference as vividly as if it was held only yesterday. "It's nonsense to see pollution in terms of Hindu or Muslim pollution," he remembered having said. "Okay ... fine ... some 4,00,000 tourists and pilgrims may be said to cause pollution for two months. But what about the pollution caused by the five million locals who stay all year around? Who pollutes the Dal Lake? Who cuts trees for making houses? And who lets raw sewage flow to our water bodies? Not tourists or pilgrims, I'm sure."

Raj had tried to apply logic, to engage in an impartial debate, to implore prevailing of common sense. But everything had backfired. He was accused by political parties of making *intemperate remarks*. And stoking *communal sentiments*. There were marches and protests in the Kashmir Valley.

There was an equally vehement reaction in Jammu. Shops remained closed for two months to enforce a virtual blockade on the movement of goods to Kashmir.

Raj was removed from his assignment and had to face an enquiry about his *vitriolic comments.* It was, in short, a royal mess all-around which lasted till the State elections were held and a new political dispensation came to power.

The present case about adoption too appeared to have the seeds of another such huge controversy.

What should I do? Raj wondered. Follow the letter of the law? Or its spirit? Apply justice blindly? Or do so compassionately? Listen to the heart? Or to the head....

The senior reader had an inkling of what Raj was thinking and opened his mouth to protest. But Raj held up his hand to silence him. "I've made up my mind. Let's go to the court."

As Raj entered the court room, everyone got up. Raj took up his seat. "I'm ruling in this case Manjoor Kumar *vs* Mehjoor Kumar. And – my decision is that Mehjoor Kumar's case be dismissed."

"Sir," Nazir Ahmed the lawyer for Mehjoor Kumar was incredulous, "but then do you propose to disregard the Shariat Act?"

"How can I disregard any law in force, counsellor," Raj responded, "but I see no way to apply a law retrospectively to an incident that took place some 27 years before that particular law came in existence."

Haji Saheb, the lawyer for the *adopted son* got up and bowed. "Your honour, even as a devout Muslim, I applaud your decision to ignore the Shariat Act. Because if you don't, thousands of cases settled in accordance with custom and practice in Kashmir would get questioned causing immense social upheaval."

Haji Saheb clapped. And as he did that, his client and his family clapped, with tears of joy and relief flowing down their cheeks. And then the whole court room clapped.

Nazir Ahmed was bewildered. But sensing the public mood, he muttered, "This is patently against the law. We will go in appeal to the Honourable High Court and get this ruling reversed."

"That's your right, counsellor, but won't you like to first collect my detailed reasoning in writing – tomorrow?" Raj smiled.

6

Delhi, 8 January 2020

IT was the turn of Air Chief Marshal Masani to explain things at the cabinet meeting.

"The Air Force has a rather small footprint in the Kashmir Valley, Sir. The main airport at Srinagar is more or less with the Airports Authority of India. We do conduct our fighter operations from there once in a while but asset-wise we just have a few facilities for the VVIPs that can be stripped down in no time."

"What about your base at Awantipora?" the PM asked.

"Our main base at Awantipora will be more difficult to dismantle, Sir. But with the D-day now firmed up, we can work backwards, co-ordinating with the army to ensure that our stores of spares, fuel etc is safely taken out of the Valley in time. We can thereafter vacate on the D-day itself, literally at a moment's notice."

"What about your other bases, Air Chief Masani?" asked the PM.

"Sir, we have a drone operation base at Manasbal which is pretty discrete in any case. So, I don't envisage any problems dismantling that facility too. Our other bases are outside the Valley, which we are not discussing at the moment, I suppose."

The PM nodded as his eyes scouted around the room.

"Any questions?"

"Masani Saheb," the Finance Minister said. "What about the financial implications, again?"

"It will be neutral, Sir. Operationally, till the D-day, our sorties will be a little more than the normal, so we'll incur more fuel costs. But afterwards, the reduced costs of transportation, storage, and security will more than compensate for the costs incurred till the D-day." Air Chief Masani paused. "However, we'll also need to be compensated for the assets left behind. Just like the army. You know Sir, for the residential quarters, schools, auditoriums, offices, guest houses, workshops that we have next to the Srinagar Airport and at Awantipora. And at Manasbal."

"That has been provided for," the Finance Minister asserted. "The 400-crore provision in the J&K Government's annual budget for sorties during natural disasters, VVIP flights, and rescue missions can more than compensate the air force for those guest houses and tacky workshops left behind. Also, just like the army, you'll be saving money on rents for the land you hold. It is around ₹ 5 crore annually, I think. So, the annual budget for the Air Force will *go up* by ₹ 400 plus 5 or ₹ 405 crore."

"That may suffice, Sir." The Air Chief nodded and proceeded to disconnect his tablet.

"Anything else," the PM queried.

"Yes Sir," Air Chief Masani started again, "as for General Hussain's apprehensions of sending us back ever again, it is not that much of a problem for the Air Force. Because whatever we are doing now, we can very well do from our other bases nearby."

"That's comforting," the PM said. "Should we move to the Navy now, Admiral Asrani?"

"Sir," Admiral Manoj Asrani acknowledged, and started his presentation.

"Sir, the Indian Navy has just a token facility at the Wular Lake, which silted as it is, is not much of a lake in any case. There will be no great problem in withdrawing our divers and other personnel, therefore, whenever the Army or the Air Force want us to do that.

"And as for the Navy's balance sheet for this operation, I think we will be quite in the green. We hardly pay a lease rent of ₹50,000 per annum for our facility at Wular Lake but spend ten times more in maintaining our personnel there. So, my boys will be more than happy to just terminate our presence in the Valley and re-join their families at Mumbai or Visakhapatnam. We don't need any compensation, therefore, from the Honourable Finance Minister."

"That's nice," the Finance Minister smiled, and stifled a yawn.

"I think, we all need a break," the Prime Minister said and got up. He moved to the table on the other end of the room where arrangements for tea-coffee stood made. The dignitaries noted that the PM hadn't ask any of the liveried bearers of the PM's office to come in and serve. TOP SECRET discussions, after all, they sighed.

The PM poured himself some Tulsi holy basil herbal tea. The Defence Minister and the Home Minister too followed suit. Others helped themselves with some strong black coffee or Darjeeling tea.

As the PM took his tea with him to the conference table, everyone did the same.

"So, where were we?" the PM asked.

"The Navy, Sir," whispered Sanjeev Chaudhury, the Cabinet Secretary.

"Oh, yes ... let's get to the next force. The BSF?"

"Right Sir," Dilip Tiwary, the Director General (DG) BSF almost stood up, and then sat down. "Sir, as the Valley has no international border but only a working LoC (Line of Control), BSF has no active border duty there. So, we are deployed just for some static guard duties like at the Raj Bhavan for the State Governor. That can be wound up quite easily, within the deadlines that your good self has indicated.

"But like every other force, Sir, we too have some facilities ... for example, at Pantha Chowk for residential quarters, messes, workshops etc ... for which, it would be nice, if the BSF could be compensated."

"What's the lease rent you're paying the State Government for all these facilities?" the Finance Minister asked.

"About a crore per annum, Sir," Dilip answered.

"Good, so that amount too we will deduct from the annual grants that we provide to the State Government and divert to the BSF. As for the structures that you have to leave behind, see whatever you can carry with you. Rest we'll have to write off, I suppose."

Dilip had one last clarification to seek. "Would it be a scorched-earth policy Sir, when we withdraw?"

"No," the PM said in a tone that stung everyone. "We'll try our best to see that all those facilities we leave behind are utilised for the benefit of the people of Kashmir who, mind you, we are not against. So, all Central Government agencies can try to minimise their losses by removing as many of their moveable assets as they can. But the immoveable assets can be left behind as they are. Is that clear?"

As no one said anything, the PM continued, "Friends, I'm NOT relishing this Operation one bit, let me clarify. But things have come to such a pass that we have to take this final step … where we separate as amicably as we can. In the process, I'd prefer we don't hurt our friends who we leave behind … and not squander away the little goodwill that we may still have in the Kashmir Valley."

"Anyway, are we done with the forces?" the PM looked at the Defence Minister and the Home Minister.

Sapru, the Home Minister spoke. "Chiman Bhai, whatever we have decided about the BSF, will apply to all our other agencies. So, the CRPF (Central Reserve Police Force), CISF (Central Industrial Security Force), NSG (National Security Guard), CBI (Central Bureau of Investigation), NIA (National Investigation Agency), R&AW (Research & Analysis wing), IB (Intelligence Bureau), NDRF (National Disaster Reserve Force) … all will co-ordinate with the Army and the BSF and ensure that we stick to the deadlines you have set for us."

"Great. We can then move to the financial implications. Ashwin?" the PM said and indicated to Ashwin Kakkar, the Finance Secretary to start his presentation.

7

Jammu, 8 January 2020

CHIEF Secretary Bashir Ahmed Fukhtoo had just reached the Civil Secretariat building in Jammu. Wearing his favourite Dolce & Gabbana sunglasses, he got down from his bulletproof Ambassador car fiddling with his walrus moustache.

He entered the building and was visibly upset to find no lift waiting for him to take him to the second floor. And the lift was stuck on the third floor. *Damn it!?*

Fukhtoo looked at Nawal, his PS (Private Secretary), who had received him at the porch. Nawal had served him for the past two years. And recently had recovered from a nervous breakdown. He had lost weight and his white shirt looked too big for his skinny torso.

"Where's the liftman?" Fukhtoo barked.

"Sir, actually just before you came, the Finance Minister had come, and the liftman had to take him –"

"Suspend the liftman."

"Pardon Sir?"

"I said suspend the liftman."

Nawal gasped for words. "But Sir … it's not really his fault."

"Then it's your fault that you didn't communicate this 'problem' to my PSO (Personal Security Officer), who could have then slowed down my motorcade … so, I would have reached when the lift was waiting for me."

"I'm sorry, Sir. I'll take care of this next time."

"You better," Fukhtoo retorted as he angrily climbed up two storeys to reach his office.

That blasted office which had no view. Just the sight of ugly flat-roofed Secretariat buildings and a crowded car park. Fukhtoo hated everything about Jammu. The weather. The crowds. The tinkling of bells and the sound of conch shells from its innumerable temples. Why, there was a temple right in the premises of this goddamn Secretariat, but no mosque as yet. And we think India is secular!

The Jammu Secretariat building had an old-world charm, admitted, but it was so bloody cramped. It had only three floors, compared to Srinagar which had five. Worse, Fukhtoo's office in Jammu, unlike Srinagar, had no walnut office table, and nil style. There was also no view to talk of, so much so that his back faced the windows.

In Srinagar, the windows were on his left, and when he looked out, he could always see the Shankaracharya, sorry Takht-i-Suleiman hill, with clouds playing hide-and-seek with the sun.

Fukhtoo despised Jammu weather because he felt colder in Jammu than in Srinagar. The ostensible reason was that the buildings here had invested more in air conditioners than room heaters. Fukhtoo had a quartz heater at his feet, and two hot air blowers at the two ends of the room. But they all burnt out the moisture in the room and made breathing difficult. There was nothing to beat the cosiness of the Turkish *Hammam* at Fukhtoo's house in Srinagar, where servants burnt wood in a cavity below his drawing room to heat its stone floor.

As he settled down in his plush swivel chair, Nawal showed Fukhtoo that day's engagements: Police DPC (Departmental Promotion Committee) meeting at 1130, lunch at 1330 with Secretary Power, Government of India, his batch mate who was in town, cabinet meeting at 1500, dinner at 2030 at the Sidhra Golf Club to bid farewell to some IAS officers who had retired over the last three months....

The engagements had to be printed on a piece of paper and put in a transparent plastic frame for *ready reference* as they called it in J&K. Fukhtoo hated computers and gadgets. So, no electronic appointment calendars for him PLEASE.

Just then, there was a knock on his door and before Fukhtoo could react, people started barging in.

"*Adab arz jenab, naya saal mubarak ho*." Greeting Sir, and wish you a very Happy New Year. The greetings were a week late, because Fukhtoo hadn't turned up for the last seven days. Even then, it appeared that the entire Secretariat had turned up to greet him. Sweepers, office orderlies, clerks, junior officers, senior officers, even some MLAs (Member Legislative Assembly) – there was no way this torrent of humanity could be checked.

Fukhtoo had to get up from his chair and shake everyone by the hand returning their greetings. Painful as it was, this was one J&K ritual even he couldn't dodge.

At 1125, the police brass headed by the DGP (Director General Police) Suresh Goyal trouped in. That was the signal for Nawal to step out and ask the orderlies to stop the crowd still trickling in to greet the 'worthy' Chief Secretary.

Fukhtoo signalled everyone to take their seats. He poured some liquid from the hand sanitizer bottle on his hands and rubbed them vigorously.

"Still scared of swine flu?" Suresh smiled.

"You bet," Fukhtoo winked, "especially as a Muslim."

Everyone guffawed at the allusion to the Islamic ban on pork, which made swine flu equally *haram*. If you could help it! It was another matter that from the time Fukhtoo was a student in the *Sainik (Soldiers) School Nagrota,* in Jammu, he had no problem enjoying booze and processed pork products like ham, sausages, and salami.

Getting to a Sainik School was another story that Fukhtoo loved to narrate once he had downed two or three pegs of whiskey. Apparently, his father was a poor farmer who could barely afford to send him to the nearest government school. But Fukhtoo was bright and his excellence in studies soon came to be noticed by Jalal-ud-Din, his maternal uncle, who was then a Block Development Officer in the State Government. Jalal offered to *adopt* Fukhtoo and send him off to a better school within or outside J&K on the condition that when he got a job, he'd marry Jalal's eldest daughter. Fukhtoo's father agreed because that would be the best way to keep his son away from the evil influence of his cousin, Ashiq Fukhtoo, who went on to marry Asifa Andrabi, the firebrand leader of *Dukhtaran-e-Millat* and was ultimately jailed on charges of murdering the noted Kashmiri Pandit human rights activist, Hriday Nath Wanchoo.

Jalal kept his part of the bargain by getting Fukhtoo admitted in the Sainik School in Nagrota where students were required to pay zilch for tuition, boarding, and lodge. All such expenses were met by the Government of India with the hope that the students of the Sainik School on passing out will join India's armed forces.

But for getting into any of those forces, you had to clear another examination conducted by the Union Public Service Commission. And you could always manage to *fail* those tests especially when you were never serious about a career in India's armed forces!

Which is exactly what Fukhtoo did. Now, after he had free schooling, he now was on the lookout for further help from the government for his college education.

Here Jalal's contacts came in handy. Soon Fukhtoo had a scholarship to fund his *coaching expenses* for getting into the IAS (Indian Administrative Service), the *crème de la crème* of Indian Civil Service. By 1986, Fukhtoo had made it to the IAS. But there was another hiccup.

Fukhtoo was allotted the Kerala cadre which meant that for most of his career in the IAS, he would be serving the State Government of Kerala instead of the State Government of J&K that he desired. That couldn't be tolerated. So, Jalal, Fukhtoo's adopted father/would-be father-in-law, persuaded the Chief Minister of J&K to write to the Prime Minister for *changing Fukhtoo's cadre from Kerala to J&K in public interest.*

The *public interest* was of keeping a Kashmiri Muslim IAS officer in J&K to help motivate more Kashmiri Muslims to join the IAS. After some dilly-dallying, the Government of India gave in. That's how, Fukhtoo escaped Kerala and landed up in J&K, where in due course he was now the Chief Secretary.

"Sir, here is the agenda for the DPC (Departmental Promotion Committee)," Altaf Kakru, the Secretary of the General Administrative Department (GAD), said.

Fukhtoo had a cursory look. Like most other officers who belonged to the State, ie the *insiders*, he too had spent all his life in J&K and so knew most officers by their first names. The agenda then was just a formality.

"Okay, Suresh. Start off."

The DGP introduced the agenda, mentioned the prescribed eligibility criteria, and explained how everyone in the suggested *Select List* was making the cut. "That's why we need to promote all five to the DGP's grade," Suresh concluded.

Fukhtoo turned towards Altaf Kakru. "GAD Secretary Saheb, any views?"

"Sir, we have only two sanctioned posts in the rank of the DGP. So, under rules, we can only promote two officers on the designated cadre posts, and two more on two non-cadre posts. So, one officer will have to be dropped."

"That won't look good," Suresh protested.

Kakru talked of the practice in other All-India Services. He then called up the Law Secretary who quoted all kinds of service law to support him.

Fukhtoo had no love lost for cadre rules made by the stupid Government of India. He knew how to short circuit this one too.

"One minute," Fukhtoo said as he got up from his chair. "Suresh come over," and both moved to his ante-room.

Fukhtoo closed the door of the ante-room. He took out his pack of cigarettes, held one to his lips and lit up. He then offered the pack to Suresh who too picked up one. Fukhtoo lit Suresh's cigarette.

Both inhaled. Fukhtoo puffed out the smoke and asked, "What's in it for us?"

"Sir, don't worry. They'll all pay. The usual rates."

And both chuckled.

"That settles it then," Fukhtoo declared and returned to his office chair.

"Secretary GAD Saheb," Fukhtoo addressed Altaf Kakru, "the decision is that we send a note to the Cabinet proposing that while we consider all five shortlisted police officers fit for promotion, we promote only these 2-3-4-5 officers to the two cadre and two ex-cadre posts of the DGP.

"And, we depute Navin, the officer at 1 to Government of India, to the Department of J&K Affairs who keep on pestering us for a competent hand. Navin's daughter is about to go to college and he has been expressing his preference for a Delhi posting for quite some time."

"Yes Sir," Kakru knew in an instant what his boss was hinting at and got up picking up his papers. He now had to make two proposals for the afternoon's cabinet meeting – one for promoting four officers, and another for 'deporting', nay deputing, one officer to Government of India.

* * *

The intercom buzzed on Fukhtoo's table. It was Nawal, his PS.

"Sir, your motorcade is ready to take you for lunch."

"Okay, guys," Fukhtoo got up, "I've to leave for another engagement," and walked to the door that was held ajar by his office peon.

Another peon was keeping the lift waiting for him. Fukhtoo hated taking the stairs even when he had to climb down. There were too many riff-raffs there who would invariably try to shake hands with him.

He got into his bulletproof Ambassador car and his four-car motorcade sped past the gates of the Secretariat. The first was the pilot-police-Gypsy with the siren hooting and a red flag waving to warn other cars *to cease and desist* from overtaking the VVIP motorcade. This was followed by one escort car with four gunmen. At number three was Fukhtoo's Ambassador. And the tail was guarded by another escort car with four more gunmen.

Within minutes, the motorcade had reached the Government Medical College and was going towards the Ranbir Canal via Bakshi Nagar. In 10 minutes, they had reached the State Guest House where Kailashnathan, the Power Secretary was staying.

8

Delhi, 8 January 2020

ASHWIN Kakkar, the Finance Secretary switched on the Bluetooth on his tablet as DG CRPF who thought his would be the next presentation disconnected his quickly.

"Sir, it is no secret that Kashmir has been a financial albatross around our necks from the time they joined India in 1947. Their annual budget nowadays hovers around ₹ 1,00,000 crore. But their revenue is just ₹ 10,000 crore. This means that we, in the Government of India, are paying for around 90% of their profligacies."

Everyone smiled as you do when you know a child has been naughty!

Ashwin continued. "Yes, the State Government has been profligate, and reckless, so much so that today their salary and pension bill is around ₹ 40,000 crore which is four times the revenues they earn. And we believe that even these figures don't tell the full story. Because the salary of daily-rated and casual workers is hidden in so many projects and programmes of the Central Government under such heads as *contingencies* or *unanticipated expenditure* that even the CAG (Comptroller and Auditor General of India) hasn't been able to ascertain the real salary bill of the State Government."

Ashwin moved to the next slide titled *Employees*. "In fact, the State has NEVER been able to tell us the total number of employees on their rolls because probably they also don't know how many of them there really are! Or, probably they don't care, because they know that India will always bail them out."

There was a lot of commotion in the room. Everyone was smiling and whispering to each other.

Ashwin grinned. "Every year, they announce a ban on recruitment of daily-rated or contractual employees and then they set up a committee to *regularise* all such temporary employees who may have completed seven years in government service. Funnily, that number ... that is the number of employees to be absorbed, keeps on increasing every year, which means that the ban on fresh recruitments was more observed in breach than in practice! It is such a racket now that the only industry operating in Kashmir today can be said to be the recruitment and transfer industry. From top to bottom, everyone only recruits people on one pretext or another or transfers them from one place to another solely for monetary considerations. Rates are fixed for each transaction, and the politicians, and their pet bureaucrats, are just raking in the riches with both their hands and feet.

"Every sector that we pick up for scrutiny reveals a racket. We have financed hospitals everywhere, but all the doctors get stationed only in Srinagar. Equipment and medicines get bought only on paper and when someone dies we only get the blame – that projects were delayed because we asked too many questions!"

"This is ridiculous," someone whispered.

"We are the Government of India, but we can't own a single inch of land there. Still, we have to pay through our noses for the land we need for running the train services for THEM, for saving THEM from disasters, for producing electricity for THEM, for running the National Institute of Technology and Central Universities THERE, for teaching THEM crafts, for running THEIR super speciality hospitals, or hospitality management and fashion technology institutes, and so on."

Ashwin paused to gauge everyone's reaction. He then moved on to the next slide.

"Coming to electricity, the so-called transmission and distribution losses there still hover around 80% which is the highest in the world! This means that the State allows people to pilfer 80% of whatever electricity they generate. And yet when it comes to maintaining old projects or constructing new ones, they always descend on us with huge, ever-enlarging, begging bowls. Every project they come up with is over-designed on purpose so that the State Electrical Engineers and their political bosses earn more commission. The result is that quite often a 100 MW hydro plant, say in Upper Sindh near Sonemarg, generates hardly 20 MW in the best of times! And this story is repeated in every project that the State has ever come up with."

The gathering watched in stunned silence as slides after slides elaborated upon the amazing lack of financial discipline in J&K.

"No doubt, Sir, India would be infinitely better off if we could shed this unnecessary 'load' as soon as possible," the Finance Secretary concluded.

"And Chiman Bhai," Sapru, the Home Minister said, "you know, for all this generosity, we are told that the militancy, or rather the terrorism there, is all India-funded? Pakistan is so bankrupt that it can't even afford to counterfeit our currency. But terrorism still flourishes in J&K because terrorists have full access to our money, our arms, and our ammunition. And even our personnel – like those boys from the CRPF – who guard the separatists? Or the SSB (Special Service Bureau) who protect their terrorist-loving ministers.

"And for all this, do you know how they treat our boys? With stones, and petrol bombs. Our *jawans* have to do duties in bunkers, for 10-10 hours at a stretch in downtown Srinagar, without even a loo break. Why? Because no Kashmiri policemen is willing to perform that thankless job. And what do they keep on hearing all around them? *Hum kya chahe Azaadi* (what we want is freedom), *Azaadi ka matlab kya, la illahi illla-lal-lah* (what does freedom mean, the Islamic rule)."

The Home Minister exhaled taking a long pause. "So, let the bastards have their *azaadi*, I totally agree with you PM Saheb."

The PM nodded and looked around the room for reactions. CabSec raised his hand.

"Yes, Sanjeev," the PM quizzed.

"Sir, we need to ask the Finance Secretary to also elaborate on what we will be losing if we abandon the Valley totally."

"Sir," Ashwin nodded. "The forces have already indicated the buildings – residential, office, workshops, auditoriums, etc, that they will be leaving behind. And we have discussed the ways we will be recovering the costs – from the savings in NOT operating from the Valley, from confiscating the State Government assets outside the Valley, from reimbursing from the outlays made in our budget for the Valley, etc.

"But there would be some other losses, hopefully only for the short term. For example, the Railways will be leaving behind their lines, yards, workshops, and station buildings, but since the State Government has NO expertise in managing these, we expect them to come to us sooner than later for help, and then we may like to come back on our terms.

"Same would be the situation with the Uri I and II and the Kishanganga hydro projects that NHPC (National Hydro Power Corporation) will be leaving behind. Again, we don't expect the State Electrical Engineers to be able to run them even for a day, because our impression is that the engineers there all forget their engineering the moment they join government service. After that, they utilise their expertise only in milking the system at the behest of their political masters. So willy-nilly, our NHPC staff too will have to be invited back, at our terms, which will benefit us financially. Even the power export and import arrangements will have to be renegotiated to our advantage hopefully.

"There will be some additional costs in maintaining our intelligence services, because I understand those operations will not be terminated. But we can house them discreetly in the accommodation vacated by so many of our other institutions like banks, insurance companies, passport centre, offices of Auditor General, Post Master General, Income Tax Commissioner, etc. So, overall I don't expect a very severe dent in our financial balance sheet from implementing *Operation Load Shedding*."

The PM turned towards Sanjeev, the Cabinet Secretary. "Any other hiccups you can think of?"

"Sir that will all depend on how smoothly we can carry out the entire exercise."

"And the secrecy we can all maintain," Sapru added, the Home Minister.

"Good, so should we now move to the internal dimensions?" the PM asked.

"Right Sir," Sartaj Daniel the NSA, responded, and started his presentation.

9

Jammu, 8 January 2020

"SIR, the Chief Secretary has moved from his office," the PSO announced who had heard the chatter on his wireless, "and should be here any moment."

"Thank you," Kailashnathan, the Central Power Secretary nodded, who was just zipping up his suitcase. That done he handed over his bag to the protocol officer who could now go to the airport to check that luggage in.

Kailash's Air India flight to Delhi was at 1500 hrs. Had he not been a VVIP, he would have had to report two hours before the flight departure time. That meant being there at 1300 hrs instead of around 1430 hrs, when he now proposed to reach the airport.

A siren's sound disturbed his reverie. *Looks like Bashir is reaching the Guest House.*

Within minutes, there were vehicles screeching to a halt, doors opening and slamming shut, heels clicking to salute the

Chief Secretary, and soon the curtains to his doors were parted.

Fukhtoo was inside the room. Without any one knocking or seeking Kailash's permission!

Kailash stood up as Fukhtoo came closer and embraced him warmly.

"How are you Kailash, and how is my old cadre?" Fukhtoo asked, alluding to Kailash's Kerala Cadre which Fukhtoo was initially allotted to.

"Oh, we are all doing fine," Kailash replied as both sat down on the antique sofa set of the State Guest House.

As the sofa set creaked, Fukhtoo could hardly hide his disgust. As everything in Jammu, he hated the Jammu State Guest House too, which looked like an outhouse of the ones in Srinagar. There were just eight rooms here, compared to the fourteen in Srinagar. And as usual, there was no view from any room, unless you thought the view of the mango orchard in the front amounted to something worth mentioning.

The rooms in Srinagar had either a gorgeous view of the river Jhelum past the mighty Chinar trees, or of the majestic Shankaracharya Hill on the other side.

Thinking of mangoes, what a messy fruit it was. The thought made him flinch. *The only fruit in which you had to put one end of the slice in your mouth, then take it out, and then put the other end into your mouth and take it out. How ungainly!*

"So Bashir, do you miss Kerala?"

"Do you mean if I miss its sambhar, fish, coconut, or its black women," Fukhtoo grunted. "Hell, nooooo."

Kailash grinned, especially at the mention of *black women* who as far as he could remember Fukhtoo didn't mind till he was in Kerala.

"Okay, so how are the white women of J&K?"

"Hey, don't mind Kailash, but you can pick up any woman from Kashmir, Jammu, or Ladakh, and they will – be all white, and very...."

Kailash flinched at the rather sexist and colourful vocabulary that Fukhtoo was using for the female population of his State.

"Any way, forget the girls. How about some drinks?" Fukhtoo asked.

And as if on cue, two liveried bearers emerged carrying some bottles of liquor, two glasses, and a pail of ice.

"It's day time, Bashir," Kailash protested.

"Okay, then have some beer." Fukhtoo opened a chilled beer can and handed that over to Kailash. "I'll have some Scotch. I've a cabinet meeting to face after lunch," Fukhtoo winked.

If Kailash was aghast, he kept his feelings to himself, as he helped himself to some spicy cashews placed in a bowl on the table.

"Have some kebabs," Fukhtoo offered.

"I think we should have lunch straight as I have a plane to catch."

"Come on, you can't escape the legendary Kashmiri hospitality when you are in my State," Fukhtoo said as he put some kebabs on Kailash's plate.

However, the bearers had in the meanwhile started laying the table. Kailash was amazed at the number of dishes being served. Looked like there were at least three mutton dishes, a chicken dish, a fish preparation in Kailash's honour, *rajma* kidney beans, *paneer*, mixed veggies, rice, and *rotis*.

Phew! Kailash finished his beer and suggested they move to the dining table. Fukhtoo finished his whiskey, poured himself another peg, and picking up his glass moved to his dining chair.

The white-gloved bearers began to serve the dishes one by one.

"What style! This can never happen in Kerala where the dominant communist culture has finished off all such bourgeois traditions," Kailash sighed.

"That's why I had to leave Kerala," Fukhtoo smiled.

"And Kailash. If you don't mind, let me turn this into a working lunch."

As Kailash nodded, Fukhtoo started off.

"You know, this issue of central power projects in our State which we have been clamouring to get our hands on."

"Yes, I've been briefed by the NHPC (National Hydro Power Corporation). But what's new about that."

"Hell, the new thing is that I'm under a lot of pressure to show some progress in this matter. Because the CM has learnt that you are not only my batch mate, but my old cadre mate."

Kailash looked up and realised that Fukhtoo wasn't joking at all.

"But Bashir, we have discussed this so many times. NHPC is a listed public company, and so they can't *gift* away any of their assets. Just like that. If your government is serious, they should evaluate the current price of those assets, and offer to *buy* it off NHPC's books. That's a simple financial exercise, and there can't be any emotion or politics attached to such an evaluation."

"Evaluation, my foot!" Fukhtoo exploded despite the rice in his mouth. "You guys have been exploiting our water resources for forty years, and you still don't want to help us?"

The phrase "exploiting our water resources" drove Kailash mad.

"Bashir, you know that's not true. Setting up a hydro project in such difficult areas requires tons of resources. And your State Government hasn't given us anything free of cost."

Fukhtoo rolled his eyes as if he wasn't listening. Which made Kailash raise his voice. "We're already paying an exorbitant lease rent to use the land. Thanks to your State Government. And on top of that, you've made our lives even more difficult by instituting false criminal and audit investigations. For projects like the Kishanganga where we've been made to pay 'compensation' to politicians and senior bureaucrats for land in Gurez valley which was never theirs."

Fukhtoo listened quietly with an annoying smirk on his face.

Kailash continued, "You have even imposed on us some 'water use charges' when you know very well that our hydro projects don't consume any water. And to make matters worse, you tell us that we've been exploiting your resources. How pathetic!"

"Calm down, Kailash!"

Kailash composed himself and then spoke, again. "If you need to take back any of our projects, the least you can do is to reimburse us the land compensation amounts that we have had to pay, and the depreciated costs of our civil structures, turbines, and other machinery that we'd be leaving behind."

"Come on, Kailash, I expected better from my batch mate."

Kailash paused for a while. "Okay, let me see what I can do," he promised half-heartedly as he polished off the last morsel on his plate and got up.

Both went up to the sink to wash their hands.

"Sorry Kailash. I'd have loved to see you off at the airport, but you know I've to attend this stupid cabinet meeting just now."

"Don't worry, Bashir. It was a pleasure catching up with you."

Both embraced, but that initial warmth was lacking.

Fukhtoo waited at the porch as Kailash got into his car and moved to the airport.

10

Delhi, 8 January 2020

"SIR, we have carefully analysed the internal implications of this Operation," NSA Daniel started his presentation, "and have reached the conclusion … there will hardly be any.

"Since 1947, we have been told that we needed to retain Kashmir because we wanted to send a message that the two-nation theory that partitioned India and created Pakistan was fallacious … that Muslims can not only survive but also thrive in a secular India.

"The 1971 war that created Bangladesh reinforced that belief … that religion alone can't be the basis of a modern Nation-State … that culture, language, traditions, food, common heritage – all play a part in defining your identity.

"Kashmir was a shining example of that culture of amity in India. And the whole of India opened its arms to welcome Kashmiris. They could buy property anywhere, but no Indian could do that in Kashmir. Kashmiri youth could work anywhere in India, but not vice versa. Kashmiris could educate themselves in any educational institution in India, but children of even IAS or army officers serving J&K couldn't have that privilege in J&K.

"All this we could tolerate. But not ungratefulness. Not this feeling of separatism. Not this idea of *Azaadi*. And definitely not these slogans in favour of Pakistan, ISIS, Sharia, and the Caliphate. It is certainly time we give Kashmiris a taste of what they have been asking for, for the last 73 years."

General Hussain, the Army Chief flinched a little at this blatantly political talk that the NSA was indulging in. But then, the NSA is a political appointee, isn't he? The General nodded at the Air Force Chief, his batch mate from their days in the NDA (National Defence Academy), who caught on what the General was thinking and nudged his colleague Admiral Asrani to let him in on the joke they were trying to share.

As Admiral Asrani winked in acknowledgement, the PM caught on the drift in NSA's presentation, and interjected, "Danielji, we have discussed these general issues so many times. It is time we came to the brass-tacks. Tell us how exactly you will implement this Operation on the ground and what co-ordination do you require from our other senior officers who are in this conference room today?"

"I was coming to that Sir," the NSA replied, and moved to the next slide.

20 slides later, the NSA concluded. "The brief point, Sir, is that unlike every other central agency operating in Kashmir we will NOT be abandoning Kashmir. Our operatives in IB (Intelligence Bureau) and R&AW (Research and Analysis Wing) will give the impression that they have wound up their operations but will actually go underground and keep on operating through our local assets.

"We have also identified those people, like Kashmiri Pandits, Indian businessmen, Indian students studying in Central Government institutions like the Central University or NIT (National Institute of Technology), on whom the local Muslims could take out their frustration ... and have worked out a schedule for shifting them out in time."

"Excuse me, Danielji," Birla, the Finance Minister spoke up, "but does that mean there will be no savings in winding up your operations?"

"Unfortunately, Sir, that is correct. Going underground and abandoning all our current office buildings will in fact increase our costs. But we can try to break even by reducing the number of our active operatives and by moving into those private buildings that will be vacated by our other brother forces like the BSF, ITBP, SSB, and CRPF. We hope and believe that our moving into such non-government buildings quietly will not be noticed by the State police and revenue agencies who will be happy taking over the larger premises vacated by the army and the air force."

Sanjeev, the CabSec broke his silence. "Mr Daniel, do we have to worry about any repercussions anywhere outside the Valley?"

"Yes, Sanjeev," the NSA acknowledged. "There will be widespread public resentment against those Kashmiri Muslims who would be there anywhere in India on the D-day, in connection with their business, employment, education, trade, or even medical treatment. We have to have, therefore, a plan in place to identify and deport them as soon as possible lest a 1947 partition-kind of situation arises."

"Danielji, this is not very clear to me," the PM interjected. "Please understand that on no count can we have a partition-kind of situation. So please think this all through."

The sharp tone stung everyone. The NSA almost lost his voice. But the PM continued, "I desire the CabSec co-ordinate all 'transfer of control' activities. He will identify a list of nodal officers in each service, State, and large metros, who will lead and control all operations in this regard. From now onwards. CabSec will also organise their briefings and trainings so that nothing is left to chance. Okay, Sanjeev?"

"Yes, Sir," Sanjeev was suddenly all ears.

"And I want this list of nodal officers on my table tomorrow, by 4 PM. Okay?"

"Right Sir," Sanjeev nodded and looked towards the other officers in the room, who all tapped awake their tablets and notebooks and started locating their list of nodal officers.

General Hussain noted that he had chosen Lt General GS Sandhu to be the GOC 15 Corps in Srinagar and nodded appreciatively. The Air Chief Marshal and the Admiral too did likewise.

"Questions?" asked the PM.

"Yes Sir," it was General Hussain.

"Yes General?"

"Sir, I was wondering ... if by accepting Muslim Kashmir as an independent nation, aren't we giving the signal that we now believe in the two-nation theory?"

"That's not at all correct, General," the NSA said. "This partition, or rather separation, is not on religious lines, but more on linguistic and regional lines. Which means – the Muslim dominant regions of Jammu and Ladakh won't join the separated Kashmir. I hope that clarifies."

"Which brings me to another point," said the PM. "Are we clear on the boundaries of this soon-to-be new nation called Kashmir? I don't want the same border mess which we had when Pakistan was created in 1947."

"Yes Sir." The NSA said as he took a few moments to project the new map of Jammu & Kashmir.

"Sir as you can see," the NSA spoke. "Even now, Jammu, Kashmir and Ladakh are three distinctly separate regions. And the boundaries of all three regions are well defined. Jammu and Ladakh have no desire to join Kashmir as they want to be with a secular India." The NSA exhaled.

"The Valley will have, therefore, a new and clear-cut border – the Banihal pass with Jammu and the Zozila with Ladakh."

Everyone nodded.

"Anything else?" asked the PM.

"Sir?" Sanjeev said.

"Yes, Sanjeev," the PM said.

"We also need to make up our mind about J&K's Chief Secretary."

"Suggest some names and show me the list tomorrow." The PM turned towards the Home Minister. "Sapru Saheb, do you have anything more to add on the internal dimensions?"

"No, Chiman Bhai. We all have the same objective in mind, which is to ensure that there is a smooth transition on the D-day. That there is no partition-type rioting anywhere, either within or outside the Valley. That all our forces are able to withdraw with NIL casualties ... and we will go all out to achieve these objectives."

"Great," the PM nodded. "Should we then move to the international dimensions? Soniji?"

"Yes Sir," Mrs Soni Ahluwalia, the Minister for External Affairs, nodded and proceeded to connect her hybrid notebook to the projection system.

11

Srinagar, 8 January 2020

AT around 6 PM, Raj Verma was back from his office, to his temporary official accommodation in the State Guest House Sonwar, which no one could call *home*. His wife, Sangeeta was in Delhi. Along with his son who was working there.

When he entered through the main door, a deep pang of loneliness hit Raj. As always.

The guest house was fully carpeted, but never vacuum-cleaned. So, its mustiness had to be tolerated for the time you had to spend in Srinagar. It also didn't help that the building had no direct sunlight streaming through. It was designed to be just cold and dark like a morgue, because otherwise, Srinagar's summer months could have been intolerable.

There were some functional, ill-matching furniture pieces in his drawing room. But no decoration items that Sangeeta loved putting in to make any government accommodation *her home*. She had a great eye for paintings, crystal sculptures, and family photos; none of which Raj had in this guest house for obvious reasons. A painful reminder that he was away from his wife and son. On a punishment posting in a god-forsaken State called 'J&K'.

Fortunately, the cooks here knew how to rustle up a few dishes: Rice, yellow dal, and cauliflower. And this was served to Raj every evening.

Raj lay on his bed and wondered what kind of life he was leading. He picked up the phone and dialled his Delhi number. Sangeeta picked up, and they began discussing each other's day. Raj mentioned that case of adoption and his moral dilemma.

"You did the right thing," said Sangeeta.

"I hope so. I don't want another controversy."

Sangeeta laughed. "As if that ever scared you. But tell me when are they making you the Chief Secretary?"

Raj sighed. "That would be a good joke."

"Come on, Raj. Don't be so pessimistic. You're next in line ... to the current Chief Secretary Bashir Ahmed Fukhtoo." Sangeeta giggled when uttering that name which brought a smile to Raj's face.

"That's only on paper. But the present government hasn't forgiven me for what happened in 2008. They still call me the villain of Amarnath."

"Yeah. But Fukhtoo will soon retire. And then as per the rules of seniority, you'll be the heir to the throne."

"That's not true," Raj said. Sadness in his voice. "I'm already hearing rumours. They're planning to circumvent the existing rules. In fact, Banarsi Das Gandotra – five years junior to me – is being promoted as the next Chief Secretary, because he is a *local boy*. The Chief Minister wants him. And she has made it clear that she does not want a Chief Secretary but a Chief Stenographer."

There was silence on the other end. Raj realised he had broken Sangeeta's heart by mentioning the painful truth.

12

Delhi, 8 January 2020

"CHIMAN Bhai," Mrs Ahluwalia started, "the international dimensions of the Kashmir problem are well-established. We all know how Nehru mismanaged the initial conflict in 1947-48 by taking the matter to the UN. And then failed to get the UN to throw out Pakistan from POK (Pak-Occupied Kashmir) to enable hold a plebiscite. Then in 1965, when Pakistan under Ayub Khan attacked India, we defeated them and captured the Haji Pir Pass that could have united both parts of J&K. But we unnecessarily went to Tashkent and on Russian pressure squandered that great opportunity by accepting the *status quo ante*. Then in 1971 we helped create Bangladesh, and held in our prisons as many as 95, 000 Pakistani POWs. But once again, we signed away all our rights through the Shimla Agreement and got zilch in return.

"And then in the 1990s, Pakistan embarked on a policy of inflicting a thousand cuts on us by diverting the battle-hardened

Taliban from Afghanistan to Kashmir. And that proxy war continues till date. Worse, Pakistan has even tried to paint us as an oppressor on the world stage that lets its Hindu majority subjugate a Muslim population in Kashmir.

"We in the External Affairs Ministry have for ages ... had a tough time explaining our stand in the international fora. But now that why we are letting Kashmiris go their own way, we think, we will gain an upper hand morally, and force Pakistan to be on the back foot to defend its exploitation of Baloochs, Pashtoons, Sindhis, and other minorities. The world will applaud India's fair-mindedness and our seat at the international high table will be reserved forever.

"Trade-wise, we will not even notice the loss of exports from Kashmir. Rampant use of banned pesticides and colouring agents has ensured that no country in the world today is willing to accept Kashmiri apple, walnut, almonds, or even its saffron. Chinese have already killed Kashmir's carpet and shawl industry by churning out clever machine-made copies. Whatever other industry is left in the Valley is focused more on the internal market, so will not be missed internationally."

Mrs Ahluwalia stopped to take a sip of water. That was an opportunity for Mr Birla, the Finance Minister to jump in.

"Soniji, what do you think of the financial implications of this operation on your Ministry?"

"Birlaji, I think it will be neutral in the short run, and positive in the long. We can't disband our Kashmir desks in some of our missions abroad immediately, but as the *Operation* gets underway, our costs associated with defending our Kashmir policy will come down. And yes, to all that, if we add the Haj subsidy too, that we won't have to shell out for Kashmiri pilgrims ... I think we will be in the green very soon."

"That'd be nice, very nice," the Finance Minister nodded.

Mrs Ahluwalia was not sure if that was a sarcastic nod because of the many run-ins that her ministry had with the finance ministry over the former's alleged profligacy or extravagance in promoting India's image abroad. But she let that pass.

"To conclude, Chiman Bhai, the External Affairs Ministry doesn't think it will have a problem defending *Operation Load Shedding*. In fact, if anything, it will only be increasing our stature in the international arena about our fair-mindedness and reassure our small neighbours that we don't covet their land."

"That's great, Soniji," the PM said. "I think that is enough briefing for today. Let's catch some sleep now, shall we?"

"Sanjeev," the PM turned towards the CabSec. "Would you now co-ordinate with your other colleagues and get me a day-by-day schedule of the *Operation* from now till the D-day? I also want the names of the personnel with their qualifications who will be leading various components of the *Operation*."

"Yes Sir," Sanjeev nodded. "I'll get going immediately."

"No Sanjeev," the PM smiled, "get some sleep first. You can show me both the lists tomorrow afternoon, around 4 PM. Okay?"

As Sanjeev nodded, the PM got up and moved towards the exit. He let Mrs Ahluwalia pass the main door first by gesturing "Ladies first." Then he waited for the Home Minister to catch up with him and walked along discussing some other matters.

13

Srinagar, 10 May 2020

FUKHTOO was glad to be back in Srinagar with the biennial Darbar Move. He loved his office room in Srinagar. And the sprawling official residence of the Chief Secretary on the banks of River Jhelum in Sonwar, the super VVIP locality. The intricate geometric shapes on the false wooden ceiling called *Qutamband,* the Kashmiri carpet on the floor, the *Chinars* all-around, the massive lawn and those beautiful roses blooming in May – he loved it all. In Jammu, his back faced the window. But here, he faced the window. Ah, that lovely view of the Takht-i-Suleiman hill from both residence and office. And the women!

Someone knocked at his door.

"Sir," it was his PSO, "Sabeena Begumji is here."

"Oh, yes … show her in."

Soon a middle-aged overweight woman sauntered in.

"Bashir Bhai," she gushed, "we meet after such a long time."

But Bashir was focusing more on the lovely Kashmiri woman in a bright red salwar kameez that was accompanying Sabeena. She was petite and had just the right look that made Fukhtoo's heart beat faster. Sabeena sure knew his taste very well.

"Take a seat," he said affectionately to no one in particular.

As the two ladies sat down on the sofa set in Bashir's drawing room, Sabeena spoke:

"This is Rafika. Rafika Hussain."

"So Rafika? Would you like some tea or coffee?"

Sabeena smiled and answered for both, "Tea please, Bashir Bhai, it is always a privilege to have tea with such an exalted personality like you."

As if on cue, tea arrived in just two minutes. Sabeena made tea for all and served Bashir first. He grabbed the cup absent-mindedly and took a s-s-s-sip.

"So Rafika, tell me something about yourself. Are you married?" he laughed.

"No, Sir, I'm not."

"And boyfriend?"

"No Sir."

"What? No boyfriend? How's that possible? No man in your life to love you?"

Rafika blushed. "No one."

"Oh! Nice. So, very nice." Fukhtoo smirked.

Otherwise it would be such a waste of a beautiful thing!

"Don't you need someone to love you?"

Rafika said nothing. She just blushed.

"Bashir Bhai, she is a poor kid who has applied for the post of a teacher in some government school and would really appreciate if you could help her out," said Sabeena.

"Indeed, it would be a pleasure," Fukhtoo said fiddling with his moustache. "I love helping young women."

Fukhtoo placed his cup on the table. "I would love to help you too. But I should get to know you better first. Sabeena ... why don't you take a walk and come back after say an hour while I conduct some background check on this lovely lady?"

And equipment checks.

While the girl looked at Sabeena quizzically, Sabeena took the hint and got up.

"Rafika, please do well in this 'interview'. I'll be back in an hour, as Saheb desires."

"Thanks Sabeena," said Bashir, "and please tell my guards outside that no one should disturb us."

"So Rafika? Why don't I show you my bedroom upstairs? Won't you like to see what kind of bed the Chief Secretary of J&K sleeps on?"

His eyes glinted with mischief.

14

Srinagar, 10 June 2020

NAFISA, a ten-year-old girl had gone missing in the forests of Rajouri. Her father, a nomad shepherd or *bakarwal*, registered a missing person's complaint in the police station. Few days later, Nafisa's badly mauled dead body was found in a ditch. The nearest house about 100 metres away was that of the priest of a small Hindu temple. The police took the body for post-mortem where after it was handed over to the family for the last rites.

*   *   *

CM Ittoo heard a knock on her office door. Her Cabinet Minister Ismail Akhtar came in and took a seat.

"Akhtar Sahib, what's the strategy?"

"Madam, you heard about that Muslim girl who was found dead in the forests of Rajouri. That area is Hindu dominated and the local MLA too is one Shiv Ram Dogra."

He then went on to explain the whole media-management strategy.

"This is explosive, Akhtar Saheb," CM Ittoo said. "No wonder, they call you my Goebbels. Now, leave no stone turned. *Yeh Khabar poore duniya mein aag ki tarah phailne chahiye. Hum Hindustan ki Sarkar ko aur uski awaam ko ghutne par le aayenge."* Make sure this news spreads like wild fire throughout the world. Let's bring the Government of India and its people to their knees.

Ismail exchanged an evil grin. "Yes Mam. Your wish is my command."

* * *

Three months later – the news indeed spread like wild fire. It was reported in the mainstream media that a few army men belonging to the *Rashtriya Rifles* had abducted a ten-year-old girl – Nafisa, and then gang-raped her. The villagers – all Hindus – joined in the gang-rape. They then took the girl to a nearby temple and ritually sacrificed her to appease Goddess Kali.

There was a national outcry, led by the left-liberal brigade, against this intolerant assault by the Hindu majority against hapless Muslims. Usually the name and the picture of the rape victim is never disclosed. But in this case, all media channels openly flaunted the name and the picture of "Nafisa, the poor Muslim girl."

Aditya Verma, a leading news TV anchor declared on his channel, "I'm ashamed to be a Hindu." Aditya Verma in the past had exposed leaders like CM Ittoo and the Hurriyat. But on this issue, he was siding with the Kashmiri leadership.

Jammu woke up aghast. Their leaders denied that Hindus or army men were behind this crime. They claimed "Hindus were being framed" but the mainstream media took that comment as "shielding the rapist."

Ultimately PM Chiman Bhai handed over the investigation to the CBI (Central Bureau of Investigation). CM Ittoo resisted this with all her might, claiming this will demoralise the J&K Police which was competent to carry out a thorough investigation on its own.

* * *

A month later, the CBI handed in its report. "There was no rape," the report established. Someone had tampered with the initial post-mortem report. Lawyers and politicians had coached 'witnesses' to claim how they heard the victim shrieking from a vehicle belonging to army/paramilitary/police (in that order of preference, please). The exhumed body had animal scratches all over, from which the girl's father too had concluded that poor Nafisa was mauled by some wild animal like a leopard.

CM Ittoo was outraged. "Shoot the rapists dead," she claimed in one of her public rallies. Entire Kashmir was up in arms, wanting azaadi, autonomy, self-rule, whatever a weak-kneed India could agree to. And the mainstream media this time – was silent. Public memory is short – so there was no problem branding this incident as a "Hindu ritual murder."

Year 2021

15

Jammu, 8 January 2021

BLAST it! Fukhtoo tossed and turned in his bed in Jammu. It was one of those lonely nights when he had to sleep alone.

And that was another thing he hated about Jammu. And its Hindu pretensions about what is right morally. Kashmiris had no such qualms. For them money came first. Then their religion. Followed by their relatives, their neighbourhood, their Kashmir, and then India.

Fukhtoo would often berate Nawal, his Private Secretary, for not being able to arrange a local girl for him. But heart of heart he knew it was not Nawal's fault. Nawal was, of course, no Sabeena. But the real reason was that local girls were so stupid that they didn't realise the benefits of spending a night with the State's Chief Secretary. And why? Because they thought their 'honour' or *izzat* was more precious than the temporary teacher's job in a government school that Nawal tried valiantly to promise them.

His mobile vibrated breaking his chain of thoughts. It was Razaq, his PSO.

"What's it, Razaq?"

"Sir, there is news that an NIA (National Investigation Agency) team has raided the Lakhanpur Toll Post."

"What? Why didn't you tell me earlier?"

"Sir, those NIA guys were so secretive that they didn't even tell their escort parties where they wanted to go. They said they wanted to go to Madhopur to try some Amritsari fish curry, but instead they stopped at Lakhanpur, and raided the cash counter there."

There was silence at the other end.

"But Sir...."

"Yes, what's it Razaq?"

"Sir, rumour is that Latif, the Excise Inspector there, has escaped NIA's dragnet and is coming here straight."

"That's good. Just go inside and get the guest room prepared for Latif."

Half an hour later, Razaq was escorting Latif inside. Latif carried two briefcases.

"Sir, these were the only two briefcases I could escape with. One is for you, and the other is for the worthy Finance Minister. I'm sorry, Sir, but I think NIA has confiscated all the remainder of *our* under-the-table income for the day."

"That's okay Latif. I suggest you lie low here till the heat subsides. And Razaq," Fukhtoo instructed, "put Latif's car in my garage and lock that. His PSO and driver too need to go underground right away. Understood?"

Razaq nodded and disappeared. Fukhtoo rang the bell, and as Bhagwan Dass his cook entered, Fukhtoo instructed him to show Latif to the guest room and serve him his dinner there.

Fukhtoo then latched up his room and opened the combination locks of both briefcases. The combination was invariably 1986 which represented Fukhtoo's batch in the IAS.

The briefcases sprang open to reveal neatly packed stacks of ₹ 2,000 currency notes. Should be a crore in each briefcase, Fukhtoo thought, which was his weekly share from the proceeds of the Lakhanpur Toll Post – the gateway to J&K, as the billboards there screamed.

Fukhtoo thanked his predecessors for their far-sightedness when they in 2017 had refused to follow Government of India's dictates for closing the Lakhanpur Toll Post. The latter were insisting that this had to be done to allow the roll out of the GST (Goods and Services Tax) framework throughout India. There were arguments galore at how such toll posts were unnecessary, how they increased the costs of doing business by increasing transport and idling costs, etcetera, etcetera. But the J&K bureaucrats had stood firm, citing their autonomy, and the constitutional provisions that enabled them to have toll posts at their border. So, the Government of India mandarins had huffed and puffed, but had then left in disgust.

But obviously they were thinking of a counter-attack. And this was it.

Fukhtoo knew what the NIA would claim, officially, which was that illegal *income* from Lakhanpur was funding terrorist activities in Kashmir, and so they had a right to raid Lakhanpur. They couldn't be faulted because it was true that Pakistan as a bankrupt country could no longer finance such activities. So, it had to be ultimately the tax payers of India who had to pay huge sums under-the-table at toll posts of

Lakhanpur to keep the fires burning in the palatial houses of the so-called separatists.

And for people like Fukhtoo, and the Cabinet Ministers, who were "closet separatists," till they were in chair. Once out of power, they would be full-time separatists, espousing the cause of autonomy, freedom, Islam, terrorism – depending on what was the flavour of that day!

16

Srinagar, 15 May 2021

RAJ Verma stood in front of his living room window staring at the rain and the dark clouds. Feeling the cold sensation on his cheeks. He could see that the Dal Lake had turned grey. And the Hari Parbat hill hidden behind the dark clouds. The rain hitting the tin roof made a soft soothing metallic ting.

It was a relief to be away from Jammu's heat. Even though Raj could do nothing about his loneliness. He hoped Sangeeta and his son were with him, enjoying the cold weather, the lake, the mountain and the rains. Except that it had rained for the past four days. Incessantly.

It was Durbar move again. The time when the State (meaning all its employees in the Secretariat) moved to its summer capital, Srinagar, in the Kashmir valley. This move had its advantages and disadvantages. The good news: you escaped severe heat of Jammu in the summer. And severe cold of Kashmir in the winters.

The bad news: You needed to maintain two houses. One in the plains and the other in the highlands. The move also meant – packing all your stuff and moving to another town just for six months and then back. Another big problem – accommodation.

Kashmiri politicians, dead or alive, had appropriated all government accommodation in Srinagar, against all rules and norms. Therefore, all non-Kashmiri employees had to be housed in hotels and guesthouses, which were often owned by these very politicians. The bills, in the name of security and national integration, were picked up by the stupid Government of India. It was a cosy arrangement all-around.

Even the senior most IAS (Indian Administrative Service), IPS (Indian Police Service), or IFoS (Indian Forest Service) officers couldn't get government accommodation in Srinagar. If they wished to live in a house, they had to hire one that belonged to those politicians who were themselves living in government accommodation in the name of security. But if they wanted to be more secure, then they had to move to the Cheshmeshahi Tourist Huts, which were mostly two-bedroom affairs with attached baths and a kitchenette.

That's why Raj Verma too, as Financial Commissioner Revenue, had landed up in hut number 208. He had chosen this hut because of its wonderful view of the sunset from its back-verandah. Also, this was the only hut with a separate servant quarter and a store room.

The only problem was its tiny kitchen, which even his cook found it difficult to operate in. So, the fridge and the microwave had to move to the dining room. Washing machine had to go to the store, invertor and batteries had to go under the front porch, and so on.

*   *   *

In the morning when Raj came out of his tourist hut, he could barely make it to his official Honda City. The rain lashed at him, ignoring his umbrella, and by the time he got inside the car, he was quite wet. Raj took the back seat and closed the door. Already the floor of the car had a few ungainly puddles of water.

Rains weren't unusual in Kashmir in April-May. They were needed for transplanting the paddy seedlings. And were much needed for the cherries in May, plums in June, and apples from September onwards.

But raining like this?

The driver started the engine, and the car moved forwards. When Raj reached Maulana Azad Road near Maisuma Bazaar, he couldn't believe his eyes. Roads were submerged under a carpet of muddy water. And the car felt like it was being driven across a mighty river. The houses on either side of the road looked more like they were overlooking a canal in Venice. But with no Rialto bridge to connect them.

The car jerked. The driver pushed hard on the accelerator but the car didn't move forward. Its wheels splashed water, and the car groaned. *I should have come in a 4 x 4 SUV.*

In a panic, the driver reversed the car and fortunately it moved.

"Sir, I'm afraid. We'll have to turn back," the driver said.

"Is there no other way?"

"No Sir. All roads appear to have submerged under water. With rains continuing, it'll probably get worse."

Raj nodded.

Raj had heard that floods had hit South Kashmir due to some overflowing tributaries of Jhelum like Lidder. There were landslides on the road to Gulmarg which were thankfully cleared up after two hours. Work on opening the route to Ladakh via Sonemarg had to be suspended.

But the rains would affect him in the heart of Srinagar? That was a little unbelievable.

The driver reversed the car and drove back to the hills of Chesmeshahi – the nearest place in Srinagar which had escaped being submerged under flood waters because of its altitude.

Just then, Raj's phone rang. It was Ajay Bansal, the Divisional Commissioner for Kashmir.

"Good morning, Sir. Sorry to disturb you so early in the morning…."

"No, it's okay, Ajay. What's the matter?"

"Sir, you know about the flood situation. I was thinking of re-energising our Disaster Control Room. Just put people there for receiving calls 24 × 7."

"No harm in that, I'm sure."

"And Sir, I was thinking of mobilising our resources of boats, inflatable rafts, SDRF (State Disaster Reserve Force) personnel, NCC cadets, etc." Bansal's tone was hesitant, which alerted Raj.

"What's worrying you, Ajay. Tell me."

"Sir, every Kashmiri tells me that we can't have floods in May in Kashmir. But if we do have that situation ever, we will have to carry out the standard drill … of cutting the Pampore bund on Jhelum so that flood waters are diverted away from Srinagar city."

Raj was silent for a moment. Yes, the drill from the time of the Maharaja was that the State Government used its flood control personnel and machinery to open the Pampore bund, a dyke about 30 km south of Srinagar. This could safely drain off substantial quantities of water to agricultural fields. The problem was that those areas today were no longer uninhabited.

"Ajay, I see no option but to be prepared for that contingency. Just ensure that it's a TOP SECRET operation, and the personnel deployed are all from North Kashmir. Anyone from nearby areas is bound to alert that terrorist politician, what's his name, yes, Mir from Lasjan, who will then certainly create problems."

"I understand, Sir. Good day."

* * *

Fukhtoo had just downed his 6th peg of whiskey. There was no party, but it was a Saturday night, and Fukhtoo had to have his usual quota of Scotch with the TV playing the 9th season of *The Vampire Games*.

"Jenab, should I lay the dinner now," the cook asked.

"Sure, Raza, do that."

Dinner over, Fukhtoo moved to his bedroom on the first floor. Usually there was a good view of the river Jhelum from his bedroom window, but that night it was all pitch black all-around.

"Bloody unseasonal rains." Fukhtoo snuggled into his comforter and dozed off.

Fukhtoo heard some screams and shouts. In his dream, he saw hundreds of women who he had once slept with – all standing in his room, and all armed with stones and canes.

Fukhtoo got out from his bed and ran outside. The army of girls chased him, throwing stones at him and hurling abuses.

It was freezing outside, and Fukhtoo was running barefoot. From the designated house of Chief Secretary in Sonwar, on to the main road, beyond the cricket stadium, beyond the State Guest House, towards the Badami Bagh Army Cantonment. People stared at him. Fukhtoo kept running till his eyes caught his bare thighs. That was when he realised he was wearing nothing. Fully naked, he was running for his life, away from his *comfort girls.*

The girls were catching up. Fukhtoo stumbled and fell. He hit the road hard, face down. The girls pounced on his back and pummelled him with sticks and stones. They slapped him and bit him. Fukhtoo whimpered, "Leave me alone, leave me...."

Someone pulled him up by his shoulders. Fukhtoo's eyes opened. It was Raza, his cook, shaking him hard to wake him up.

"Jenab, I think, Jhelum has breached its bund somewhere. Please wake up."

Fukhtoo got up with a grunt sound.

The room had no light. "Why don't you switch on the lights?"

"Sir, I can't because there's no electricity."

"No electricity, eh? In the Chief Secretary's house?"

"Jenab, the grid has tripped ... and our back-up system on the ground floor is flooded. So, we have disconnected that."

"Bloody hell!" Fukhtoo wore his cardigan over his sleeping dress. He was glad he wasn't naked. He moved towards the window.

The view was nothing like he had ever seen before. There was water all-around. If he could sit on the window ledge, Fukhtoo could dip his toes in the water. That meant his entire ground floor, the carpets, paintings, kitchen stores – everything was submerged.

Fukhtoo panicked, as he staggered back from the window. Raza caught him and made him sit on the bed.

"Jenab, our guards have already informed the Control Room. Help should be reaching us soon."

At 0300 hrs, Fukhtoo thought he heard the sound of an approaching motorcycle. But fortunately, that turned out to be an inflatable SDRF (State Disaster Relief Force) boat fitted with a Honda outboard motor reaching his house. It circled the house once as Raza flung open his window and shouted and waved his hands. The boat immediately made its way to the window.

"Chief Secretary Saheb, please step out of the window and slide down," a voice shouted.

Fukhtoo did as advised. His legs were still unsteady. But Raza helped him climb on to the window ledge, dangle down his legs, from where someone pulled him down, rather rudely and unceremoniously.

The boat sped to the Gupkar Road, where on higher ground, vehicles were waiting. Eager hands helped Fukhtoo out of the boat and helped him get into a government SUV which drove a kilometre to reach Hari Niwas, the Government Guest House, next to the Grand Hotel.

Fukhtoo was still in his pyjamas as he climbed up the stairs of the Hari Niwas to reach his room. The wall clock on the way showed 0330 hrs.

17

Srinagar, 16 May 2021

SOMEONE was knocking persistently. Fukhtoo woke up with a start.

"Who is it?" He tried to shout, but what came out was a croak. Looked like he had caught a chill last night.

The knocks continued. So, Fukhtoo dragged himself up, staggered to the door, and flung it open. A skinny man was standing, his uniform indicating he was a bearer of the State Government's Hospitality and Protocol Department.

"Yes, what do you want?"

"Sorry Sir, but the Honourable CM Sahiba has just sent a message that she wants to hold a meeting with you and other senior officers at 11 AM here."

Fukhtoo sighed. He covered his sleepy eyes with his hands. *Damn CM?!* "Okay, I'll be there."

He moved to his bed to lie down again. Something felt different. His mattress wasn't comfortable. The orientation.... Even the floor seemed unfamiliar....

That's when it hit him – that he was not in *his* house but in Hari Niwas. And then he remembered the horror of the night, the swirling, black, flood waters, his getting on to a wiggly raft, et al.

"Ahhh …" Fukhtoo caught his head to soothe his splitting hangover. He looked for his favourite painkillers but they were not there at his bedside table.

Oh, those blasted floods.

Fukhtoo stumbled across to the wardrobe and flung it open. His clothes weren't there – especially his suit.

That idiot Raza, Fukhtoo swore again, *how dare he pack me off without even a change of clothes?*

His eyes fell on the intercom on the side table. He lifted the handset and was surprised to hear a dial tone.

Okay, so the bastards are running a generator here. He was relieved.

Fukhtoo pressed '0' for reception and someone answered immediately.

"*Jenab*, Sir? How may we help you?"

"Listen, is Raza my attendant around?"

"Let me check, Sir," the operator said. Fukhtoo heard him shouting Raza's name in the background, and then he heard, "Yes, Sir. He is here. Should I send him up?"

"Yes, please." Fukhtoo put the receiver down with a bang.

Within minutes, Raza was at Fukhtoo's door. He was blabbering about where all the flood waters had spread, who all were rescued, when Fukhtoo raised his hands to silence him.

"Raza, go home. Pick up my clothes, my shoes, and yes, my toiletries and medicine kit, and be here within 20 minutes, max, okay?"

Raza nodded. So, Fukhtoo made him repeat what he had asked him for. He knew Raza was not immune to the charms of the same hard liquor as he was. But Raza could repeat his demands verbatim, which was a relief.

As Raza turned back, Fukhtoo shouted, "And Raza, tell the dining room boys to send me some omelette and black coffee ... please. Okay?"

Raza nodded and ran down the stairs.

* * *

Sunlight was entering Fukhtoo's bedroom. He was still groggy, but he had to get up.

Fukhtoo staggered across the bathroom to freshen up. There were okay toiletries there. The towel too smelt all right. When Fukhtoo came out, his breakfast was waiting on the small dining table in his suite.

When Fukhtoo lifted the cloche, he was horrified. There was no omelette. Instead there were four cold *pooris,* that blasted Indian puffed bread that Fukhtoo hated, and some boiled potatoes floating in a flood-water gravy.

"What the f***," Fukhtoo swore, as he heard a knock on the door.

It was Raza carrying his stuff, which he hastened to put in the wardrobe.

"Wait, Raza. Is this what I had asked you to order?"

"Sir, I'd ordered omelette as you had asked for, but the kitchen said they'd received no supply of eggs and bread today. And whatever little they had in stock, they had already used up for other guests. So, they could only rustle up some *poori-sabzi*."

Fukhtoo gave him a blank stare, but Raza was now putting Fukhtoo's toiletries in the bathroom, and the medicines inside the drawers of the bedside table.

"Sir, which shoe should I polish? Black or the brown."

Fukhtoo was in no mood to wear a suit. Brown would then be somewhat informal.

"Brown."

As Raza got down to polishing the brown shoes, Fukhtoo gave the *pooris* a try. They were cold, and hard, and dripping with oil. After a few morsels, Fukhtoo gave up in disgust, and got up to change from his pyjamas to something more appropriate.

* * *

At 1105 hrs, CM Hasina Ittoo got out of her car and stared at that white building with green tin roofs – the infamous Hari Niwas that was once supposed to be the palace of the Maharaja of Kashmir. As she climbed the stairs, her eyes fell on the paintings and the severed heads of stuffed animals that hung from the walls. The palace looked quaint and serene but Hasina was well-conversant with its horrible history.

During the 1990s (early years of militancy), this building housed the CID (Criminal Investigation Department) Headquarters and its infamous *interrogation* or rather torture chambers. Many terrorists succumbed to their injuries here, and it was believed their restless souls still haunted this building. One look at the severed head of a leopard with open jaws – and the thought of ghosts made Hasina shudder.

In any case, there was a popular belief that whosoever stayed in this building lost his chair. Hari Singh, the last Maharaja of Kashmir, had got this imposing palace built during his reign. But before he could spend any time here, J&K had to accede to India, and the Maharaja was banished to Bombay to die like a commoner in an alien land.

Mufti Mohammad Sayeed decided to turn this building into a museum and got his cabinet to endorse the idea wholeheartedly. But his successor Ghulam Nabi Azad, the Congress party Chief Minister, was greedier. He scrapped the museum idea and shifted his (that is the Chief Minister's) official residence here. But the 2008 agitation related with the Amarnath Yatra claimed his chair. After that, no Kashmiri ruler could think of staying here and this building thereafter served as a guest house for senior government functionaries from Delhi who knew little about its inauspicious reputation.

* * *

By 1107 hrs, Hasina had reached the dining room, which was quickly converted into a conference room. There was a flurry of movement as officers got up from their chairs. A chair toppled in the process.

Hasina noticed that the Chief Secretary was present although in a casual attire.

Thank God, he's not in his pyjamas, in which he was rescued last night. Hasina sniggered, as she motioned all to take their seats.

"Bashir Saheb," she barked at the Chief Secretary, "what's the latest?"

"Madam ... I've just been briefed that half the city is under water. Rajbagh, Shivpora, Jawaharnagar, are all inundated up to the roofs of their ground floors. Our Secretariat also is under ten feet of water. Police Control Room is functional. Bansal, the Divisional Commissioner is there co-ordinating rescue efforts, but even he can't get out of that building –"

"What about any help from the Centre?"

Why ask the Centre for help? What happened to your great idea of self-rule, Madam?

But Raj Verma controlled his thoughts and spoke, "Madam ... I was able to contact DG NDRF (National Disaster Reserve Force) and he's flying out a special team today. I have requested him to get some satellite phones too as our mobile network in absence of electricity is about to collapse. He says he will be able to manage some 80 sets, so we'll have to be ready with a list of officers who would be authorised to use these sets."

"And Madam," Fukhtoo intervened, "if we get those satellite phones, we will also have to fix some financial limits on their usage as the call rates on these sets are quite exorbitant."

"Let's not worry too much about the rates," CM Ittoo said, "as our priority is to save lives. We can always prevail upon the PM of India to bail us out later."

Raj flinched at the reference to "the PM of India."

The Home Secretary sitting next to Raj whispered, "Great, why doesn't the lady try to get something from the PM of Pakistan too. For the people of Kashmir for a change. And not for her own coffers."

"Okay, what about the Indian Army? Have they come out of their burrows to help flood victims?" CM Ittoo asked, hinting at the army's pre-occupation with saving their men and stores in Badami Bagh cantonment which was the first to be flooded.

"Madam," Hafiz, the Tourism Secretary spoke. "We don't really need them. Our *shikarawalas* are already doing a better job of saving lives than the Indian Army."

"Yes, but at what cost?" Fukhtoo asked sarcastically. "I'm told their rates are pretty usurious nowadays. And if you don't have cash, then you are expected to part with your jewellery for getting a ride to higher grounds. After all, there is no such thing as a free boat ride. Isn't it?" Fukhtoo fiddled with his moustache and grinned.

Raj looked at Hafiz's face which had dropped. "I take strong offence to this comment." Hafiz's tone was steady. "If there are a few bad eggs, let our police arrest them. Doesn't mean they are not doing a difficult job?"

Bastard, CM Ittoo mused under her breath. *Just because the shikarawalas owe their allegiance to the opposition party, the Tourism Secretary is trying to save their reputation, as if they have any. They'll need to be taught a lesson, but some other day.*

"DGP Saheb," CM Ittoo ordered, "please ensure that such exploitative behaviour is not tolerated anywhere."

"Yes, Madam," Suresh answered. "We will do that. Fortunately, the Police HQs, being on higher ground at the Airport Road, is functional. But most of our residences, including mine in Sonwar, is under water. We are trying to contact all policemen and putting them on duty. The situation in Jammu –"

"Sureshji," Fukhtoo interrupted. "Let's focus on Srinagar first, where the situation is much more serious. We will come to Jammu next week."

Ah, the eternal communal angle ... let us save the Kashmiri Muslims first, and let the Jammu Hindus fend for themselves, Raj mused.

The PS to CM suddenly rushed in with a phone for the CM. Hasina raised her hands to shut everyone up as she took the call. "Yes TSR, you can give me the line now."

Everyone fell silent as apparently that was the PM's Personal Secretary on the other end.

"Sir," CM Ittoo screeched. "*Haalat bahut kharab hai yehan.*" The situation is really bad here.

And she proceeded non-stop for the next five minutes haranguing the PM. That included a lecture on how the Indus Water Treaty that India signed with Pakistan in 1960 had harmed Kashmir so much and how that also had to be blamed for the current floods.

Suddenly her face fell. "Day after tomorrow? PM Saheb? As you wish."

As she disconnected the phone, she turned towards the gathering. "The Indian PM wants to see things for himself tomorrow, no day after tomorrow, which is 18 May. So be ready. His PS should be communicating the detailed programme soon to the Chief Secretary. Let's focus on that now full-time." She paused.

"Okay, that will be all for today." Hasina got up.

I better go and touch up my hair today.

18

Hari Niwas, Srinagar, 16 May 2021

EVERYONE stood up in the dining-cum-conference room as CM Ittoo left. The meeting was far from over for Fukhtoo as he now had to plan for the PM's visit. So, he motioned all officers to stay put as he saw off the CM.

"Okay, so where is our damage assessment report?" Fukhtoo asked getting into the chair in the centre that the CM had just vacated.

"I've checked up with the Divisional Commissioner, Kashmir, and he says he is still compiling it," replied Raj.

Seeing Fukhtoo grimace, Raj continued, "I think I'll co-ordinate it all from the Revenue Administration's side and will try to have something ready by 5 PM today, if that be okay, Bashir."

He saw the look on Fukhtoo's face and realised that Fukhtoo didn't like being called by his first name in public. Especially by him. But Raj couldn't help it. Being just one batch junior to Fukhtoo that is how Raj had addressed him his entire life.

"No, Raj. That won't be okay. I need inputs from all departments, and not just Revenue ... so I think it's better to let the GAD Secretary compile all the data. You needn't worry."

Raj understood instantly what Fukhtoo was hinting at. Being the head of the Revenue Administration, Raj and his subordinates, ie the Divisional Commissioners, the Deputy Commissioners, the Tehsildars, down to the Patwaris were the best people to compile a damage assessment report. But now Fukhtoo had obviously decided to side line him so that Raj became 'less-important'.

Fukhtoo looked at others and barked, "By 5 PM, the fully compiled report should be on my table. I'll request the Honourable CM to hold a Cabinet Meeting by 6 so that I can brief the Cabinet all about our estimates, projections, demands ... whatever we will be submitting to the Indian PM day after tomorrow. Secretary GAD should keep his staff ready to print, photocopy and bind enough copies of the report from around 8 PM onwards. Is that clear?"

There was silence in the room as his detailed instructions surprised everyone.

"Sir?" Altaf Kakru, the Secretary GAD, broke the silence.

Fukhtoo rolled his eyes. "Yes, Altaf. What is it?"

"Sir, the Secretariat is under ten feet of water. So how will we reach my office?"

"Oh! So, do I have to find a boat for you now?"

Sensing Fukhtoo's mood Raj intervened. "My office is not under water." He paused. "So Altaf, you're welcome to use our facilities –"

"No, Altaf." Fukhtoo cut him off immediately. "Make a temporary office here, in Hari Niwas, so that I can personally supervise the whole operation. Do whatever is required to make this office fully functional. Ask the NIC (National Informatics Centre) to rig up an internet connection, shift some computers, printers and photocopiers from your office, and let's get cracking. *Koi shaq?"* Any doubts?

"No Sir," Altaf nodded.

"Anything else?" Fukhtoo looked around the conference room.

"Yes," Raj spoke again.

Fukhtoo gave another disapproving glance. "What's it, Raj?"

"Just wanted to know who all would be required at the airport day after tomorrow to receive the PM?"

"I think I, the DG (Police), the Planning and Finance Secretary, along with the CM should be enough."

Raj understood what Fukhtoo was trying to convey. He being the second senior most officer after Fukhtoo should have been included in the team to receive PM Chiman Bhai. But Fukhtoo was ensuring that Raj remained side-lined. Hidden from the gaze of the PM for whatever reason.

"Bashir, the tradition in the State is that whenever a dignitary like the President or the Prime Minister visits the State headquarters, the entire cabinet and the senior officers up to the level of Principal Secretaries are lined up at the foot of the ladder of the VVIP aircraft and are introduced to the dignitary." Raj paused. *That includes me.*

"These are extra-ordinary times, Raj," Fukhtoo interjected, "and it will really look odd if we went with a *baraat* (marriage procession) to greet the Prime Minister as if everything were normal. Okay? Now let's get to work."

Fukhtoo got up and moved to his room upstairs.

* * *

Raj went back to his office on his 4 × 4 Mahindra Scorpio through the *Habba Kadal* route which was wadable. There was no one in office except for his orderly and a clerk. His eyes fell on his office landline. The only landline which was working. He realised he hadn't spoken to Sangeeta since the mobile phone towers had stopped working. He picked up the landline and dialled Sangeeta's mobile number.

Sangeeta picked up the call and was unstoppable.

"Thank God, you called. Otherwise I was so worried. On television, they're showing that the whole Kashmir Valley has gone down under water. Is it really this bad?"

"Yes, it is. But fortunately, my hut in Cheshmeshahi and my office near Habba Kadal – both being on higher grounds are unaffected," Raj said.

Sangeeta was breathless asking him about his welfare. Whether he was eating right, sleeping properly and looking after himself. "I've heard the PM is visiting Kashmir soon. You must be busy."

"I'm afraid I'm not." Raj could only muster this much.

"What do you mean you're not? You head the Revenue administration and are second to Fukhtoo in seniority."

"Yeah. I think that's where the problem lies."

There was silence at the other end. And then Sangeeta's voice came back. "What do you mean?"

Raj sighed. "He hasn't included me in the team to receive the PM day after tomorrow."

"What?" Raj knew Sangeeta would react like this.

"He hasn't even let me or my office compile the damage assessment report."

"But … this is ridiculous."

"It is. He's acting paranoid. He's behaving as if the PM would see me and immediately make me the Chief Secretary replacing him." Raj paused. "Why he doesn't even like if I address him as Bashir."

"Then call him Fukhtoo. In any case, he's living up to his surname," Sangeeta broke into a laughter.

That's what Raj loved about Sangeeta. Even in tense situations like this, she had this knack to joke and bring a smile to his face.

19

PM's Visit, Srinagar, 18 May 2021

THE rains had stopped, but the sky was still full of dark clouds. There certainly appeared to be no possibility of the sun god smiling anytime soon.

But there appeared to be every possibility of the PM's special Air Force aircraft making it to Srinagar. Fukhtoo sighed as he looked out of his window. Any other time, he would have enjoyed the view of the clouds hovering over the serene waters of the Dal Lake, but today he was distracted.

Just then the intercom buzzed.

"Sir, the State helicopter is ready to transport you and your group to the airport." Fukhtoo's PS had called.

"Great," Fukhtoo acknowledged. "I'll just come down."

Fukhtoo looked at himself in the mirror, and thought he looked good in his imported Harris Tweed jacket, matching trousers, and shoes. He gave a last-minute tug at the knot of his flaming red tie and rushed down the stairs.

As Fukhtoo got down into his car, his PS gave him three copies of the *Interim Damage Assessment Report of the Flood Situation in Jammu and Kashmir: May 2021.* Fukhtoo flicked through the pages and came to the summary. The total indicated was ₹ 10,000 crore.

And that was the 'interim assessment' as the report declared. Depending on the PM's mood then, J&K could add as many zeroes as they wanted.

In 3 minutes, Fukhtoo's motorcade had crossed the Raj Bhavan's security and was entering the Nehru Helipad. The Principal Secretaries of Finance and Planning Departments were already waiting, 'as desired' by Fukhtoo. The fourth passenger that day was the Principal Secretary to CM. He must have been told to come by the CM, Fukhtoo thought.

Fukhtoo shook hands with the pilot and the co-pilot who were ready to start the engine. They first guided the passengers to board. The pilots ensured that all four had fastened their seatbelts, including the Chief Secretary, who was a little lax about all such security precautions.

Within moments, the rotors were whirring, and the chopper took off. It languorously flew over the Royal Springs Golf Course and then over the Dal Lake. Fukhtoo could see how the entire Boulevard was still under three feet water. There was water all over the Kashmir Golf Course, Lal Chowk, Jawaharnagar … till they approached the airport which was wet but not flood-affected.

The chopper dropped them at the Technical Area and flew back to pick up the CM. Fukhtoo and the officers walked over to the Indian Air Force's VVIP Guest House where the local Station Commander received them.

Just then an army chopper landed and out came the Corps Commander. Badami Bagh too was under water, and so from where had the Corps Commander managed to board this army chopper, Fukhtoo wondered.

As tea and cashew nuts were served by the smartly turned out staff of the Air Force Guest House, CM's entourage also landed. Fukhtoo kept his cup of tea aside and rushed out to receive the CM.

A look at Fukhtoo and CM Ittoo raised eyebrows indicating she didn't much approve of the way the Chief Secretary was dressed that day. As if he was going to a party. He should have been in the customary black *bandgulla* (closed-neck jacket) that CM Ittoo thought was the prescribed dress code for such occasions. But now it was almost 0850 hrs. Too late to get that blasted *bandgulla* for the Chief Secretary.

* * *

At 0858 hrs, Prime Minister's Boeing 737 touched down. It rolled down the entire length of the runway, then turned back and sauntered towards the Technical Area.

As the ladder moved towards the craft's front door, the local dignitaries lined up. First, was the Air Force Station Commander, not because he was the senior-most, but because it was *his* station. Then came the CM, followed by her three senior-most ministers. After that was the Chief Secretary, the Corps Commander, and so on.

The moment the crew inside signalled that everyone was in place to receive the PM, they flung open the door and stood aside. Dressed in a brown *Khadi bandgulla*, the PM stepped out first. As the Air Force Station Commander saluted him, Hasina Ittoo stepped out of the line to greet the PM effusively and to present an exquisite bouquet of roses. That was the signal for other ministers who all milled around the PM to shake his hand and do *Adaab arj* (literally salutations are presented). The SPG (Special Protection Group that protects the PM) had a tough time letting the PM continue to meet other dignitaries in the 'line-up'.

"Where did she manage that from?" Fukhtoo whispered in Iqbal's ears who was the Principal Secretary to the CM. *When most people have lost everything including their clothes?*

Iqbal stared at Fukhtoo as if he were an imbecile. "Oh, the bouquet? Of course, from the Grand Hotel where there always is a functional florist."

By then, the PM had reached Fukhtoo who introduced himself as the Chief Secretary. He did the same to the Home Minister, the Cabinet Secretary, and the Director IB who were following the PM.

Formalities over, the entire entourage trooped to the VVIP Guest House where they made themselves comfortable.

"Patel Bhai, we are so grateful," CM Ittoo said, "that you could visit us at such short notice. And Home Minister Saheb, I thank you too for coming along. You must have seen how devastated we have been by this terrible, horrible flood. Most people have lost their homes, and all their life's savings. India must go all out to compensate us...."

The PM was quiet and let Hasina blabber on nonstop for almost three minutes. Then when she paused to catch her breath, he commiserated, "Yes Hasinaji, I had a look from the air. And I do find the situation terrible. But tell me, what really happened? Did some dam or reservoir suddenly give way? Was there some cloud burst somewhere high up in the hills ...?"

Fukhtoo tensed up as he knew what the PM was hinting at. No unexpected calamity had taken place anywhere in the Valley. No hurricane, tornado, or even the monsoon had assaulted Kashmir. What had happened was that it had rained for five days – normal, Kashmir style peter-patter rain. But the waters couldn't be drained off because all-natural outlets had been either blocked or encroached upon – not by Indians, or Pakistanis, but by true-blue blooded State-subject Kashmiris. For all practical terms, therefore, this was a man-made tragedy, and here was the J&K CM asking the Indian PM to 'compensate' her for her mis-governance!

But Hasina refused to take the hint. She was unstoppable. She snatched the copy of the *Interim Damage Assessment Report* that Fukhtoo was carrying and presented that to the PM as if that were another bouquet.

"Look Sir," she screeched, "our brilliant officers have come up with an initial assessment. And it already touches ₹ 10,000 crore."

The PM took the copy in his hands and casually turned the pages. The report had listed damages sector-wise and suggested preliminary estimates to repair them. He passed it over to the CabSec.

"Sanjeev, please get this examined by the NDMA (National Disaster Management Agency) and see what all we can do."

The CabSec nodded and took the copy. That was the signal for Fukhtoo to unburden his load and he handed over three more copies to Sanjeev.

"But Bashir ...?" Sanjeev asked. "Won't you be making some kind of presentation first?"

"I'd have loved to, Sir," Fukhtoo answered, "but this is Air Force territory. I wish you could come down to our office, or at least to the Hari Niwas where we are staying temporarily, and I would have been happy to make a detailed PowerPoint presentation."

"Okay, but just clarify a point," Sanjeev asked, "which is: have you made these estimates in line with the national norms? You know, NDMA guidelines ... that only provide relief for temporary restoration, and those sums are the same whether a disaster takes place in Kerala or in Kashmir."

"We will do that Sir," Fukhtoo replied. He knew what the CabSec was hinting at, which was that we don't finance your *shopping lists*. So, don't ask for 'compensation', which is what is given out by insurance companies, provided you have paid some premium to insure your assets. Government of India only gives 'relief', as per set norms, to help tide over some hardships.

So, if an electric transformer is burnt down, Government of India can help you re-route the power supply from some other area so that people don't suffer. But it will not finance the purchase of a new transformer. Similarly, if someone dies, the Government will give some token amount to help meet his funeral expenses but will not 'compensate' for his lost earnings. And so on.

Most politicians didn't know that subtle difference between 'compensation' and 'relief'. But Fukhtoo knew what was expected and promised that a new document, in accordance with the prescribed all-India 'relief' norms would be on the CabSec's table in two days.

And yes, he will come down to Delhi personally to make a proper presentation to the CabSec and the NDMA.

Meanwhile hot tea and khakhras (a Gujarati savoury) were served to the delegation. PM had a sip and got up.

"Hasinaji," he addressed CM Ittoo. "Let's do an aerial recce before the weather turns bad."

And before a flabbergasted CM Ittoo could reply, the PM walked back to the Mi-17 which was waiting for him in the Technical Area.

Soon the CM and her three Cabinet Ministers were airborne with the PM. For half-an-hour, they flew over the Valley from Srinagar to Baramulla to Ganderbal to Pampore, roughly the area that was under water. By 0945 hours, they were back in the Technical area.

"See I told you the situation is bad," CM Ittoo said. Her tone almost aggressive. The PM cocked his head towards her.

"Prime Minister Saheb, you'll have to help us. You'll have to compensate us. India has no option. We, Kashmiris, made a major decision to join India in 1947. We could have gone with Pakistan. Or with China. We had the choice, but we chose you. We took bullets. Our women became widows. And now this flood has devastated the average Kashmiri. You'll have to do at least this much for us." She paused. "This is what you owe us."

The PM said nothing. But his looks made it obvious that he didn't like CM Ittoo's tone. Or her words. She spoke as if she or her people had done a favour to India in 1947.

* * *

By 0950 hrs, the PM had boarded his Boeing 737, and within minutes they had taken off from Srinagar Airport. There was a little turbulence over the Banihal Pass which was expected. But once outside the Valley, the aircraft climbed to its cruising altitude of 30,000 feet and was purring along comfortably on its way to Delhi.

The moment seatbelt signs were switched off, the PM got up from his seat and moved to the conference table. He motioned the Home Minister, Cabinet Secretary, and the Director IB to join in.

There was an uneasy quiet for about a minute. And then, the PM spoke.

"Sapru, you're a Kashmiri too. Tell me why I feel as if I was insulted today?"

"Chiman Bhai, don't take it personally. That's how Kashmiris are. Sometimes they forget the PM is visiting them, and that they have to conduct themselves professionally."

"And what was that? Thrusting a ₹ 10,000 crore shopping list in my hands as if our only purpose in life is to give out doles?"

"As I said, Chiman Bhai, these guys are a little crude, but…."

It was difficult to defend Hasina, Sapru sighed. She had always been a strong advocate of self-rule, whatever that meant. But had no qualms waving a shopping list at our faces when she got a chance.

"No, no … I'm not talking of the CM alone. I can understand that she has no control over her tongue. But what about her Chief Secretary? He thinks he can add as many zeroes as he feels like and we will just pay up?" There was rising anger in PM's tone. "Isn't he a direct-recruit IAS officer? What's his name?"

"Bashir Ahmad Fukhtoo, Sir," both the CabSec and the Director IB replied in chorus.

"What?" the PM rolled his eyes as if he couldn't believe what he was hearing.

"Chiman Bhai, it is a simple Kashmiri surname," Sapru smiled, "and it doesn't mean what you're thinking. In Kashmiri at least."

"Sir," Director IB said, "but his dossier is full of incidents that quite live up to his name in English."

"I'll certainly like to have a look at that dossier. But tell me why was this Fukhtoo fellow not ready for a proper presentation?" The PM was still upset.

"Sir, that's how he is. A little laid back. And that's how he has always been from the time he got into the IAS and was allotted the Kerala cadre," Sanjeev explained.

"Okay, so you all think they were not deliberately insulting me even though I didn't like the way the CM made her case. And … those zeroes in the report. I'm not convinced. But now I'm even more determined to launch our *Operation Load shedding.*"

"There is no other option, we agree," Sapru nodded.

"Yes, but there is no way I can include this Fukhtoo fellow in our *operation*. Sanjeev, I thought I had asked you for a panel of officers from which we could select a more suitable Chief Secretary to head J&K during this transitory phase?" the PM asked.

"Yes Sir, you had. And we are ready. Whenever you desire, Sir, I'll come down to brief you," Sanjeev answered.

"I don't want to delay this. Let's do this today, say around 4 PM?"

"Yes, Sir."

"Sapru Saheb, could you also join in?"

"Certainly, Chiman Bhai. I'll just ask my staff to re-schedule my afternoon appointments."

Just then, the pilot requested the VVIPs to return to their seats and fasten their seat belts as they would be landing shortly.

* * *

At 1555 hrs, Sanjeev Chaudhury got out of his office from the President's Estate and five minutes later was in the PM's office in the South Block. Sapru was already in. They were discussing the political situation in Gujarat, Sanjeev thought, but clammed up when they saw him enter.

PM gestured Sanjeev to sit down, who placed the folder he was carrying on the PM's desk, before taking his seat.

PM flicked through the five pages, each containing a photo and a short bio-data of a senior J&K cadre officer, who was in the 'zone of consideration' for the Chief Secretary's post. He then passed over the dossier to Sapru and looked up.

"Sir, these are the five senior-most officers of J&K. The first suitable officer is Raj Verma, who is a rung junior to

Fukhtoo, the current Chief Secretary. He is currently the Financial Commissioner (Revenue) and head of the revenue as well as the disaster relief machinery," Sanjeev said.

"Was he there at the airport?" the PM asked.

"No Sir," Sanjeev answered, "because Bashir feels a little threatened by Raj Verma … he didn't want you to meet or get impressed by him."

"Hmmm … who are the others?"

"Sir, the next three in order of seniority are all in Delhi, in various ministries…."

"Okay. Who is the fifth officer then?"

"Sir, he is five-years junior to Raj. He is still not in the pay grade of the Chief Secretary as the other four officers senior to him are. But he is a local, belonging to Jammu, with excellent contacts in political circles."

"Since when has that become a criterion for becoming the Chief Secretary?" The PM turned towards Sapru. "What do you think?"

"I know Chiman Bhai," Sapru said, "what the CabSec is hinting at. On seniority or competence, Raj Verma should be our number 1 choice. But remember, he was the CEO of the Amarnath Shrine Board in that 2008 Amarnath controversy. When the entire J&K was locked down for two months? In that background, Raj will be the least acceptable Chief Secretary to the Kashmiri leadership. That's why the CabSec has included a junior Jammu boy in this list."

"Come on, Sapru Saheb. That was the crisis which got our party's local unit in power in Jammu. So why should we ignore this officer? In any case, wasn't he just doing his duty when the so called Amarnath crisis erupted?

"But forget all that 12-year-old history. For our forthcoming *operation,* tell me, who should we trust more?

This fellow Raj Verma or that politically acceptable Jammu boy?" the PM asked.

"Raj Verma any day," Sapru and Sanjeev said in unison.

"Raj is a nationalist to the core. The only thing is that sometimes he is too stubborn when he is asked to bend rules," Sanjeev added.

"That is okay. But tell me, when it comes to the crunch, will he carry out a clear-and-direct order?"

"Yes Sir," Sanjeev assured, "with his life, if that be in the national interest."

"That settles it then. Sapruji, operationalise our change-Chief-Secretary-mission then. Choose a date, but don't delay it beyond a month."

20

Srinagar, Friday, 11 June 2021 (1)

THE AGM (Annual General Body Meeting) of the J&K Tourism Development Corporation (JKTDC) had just concluded. Fukhtoo being the Chief Secretary was in the chair. Everyone was now proceeding to the banquet hall on the first floor of the Sher-i-Kashmir International Convention Centre (SKICC) for lunch.

Fukhtoo's eyes lit up when he saw at least twenty-five mutton, fish, and chicken dishes being served. A complete *wazwan* buffet. His gaze fell on Hafiz, the Tourism Secretary, who was handing over a plate, spoon, and a napkin to him.

Fukhtoo accepted the plate and grinned.

"Can't imagine," Fukhtoo flashed his teeth, "that only a month back the floods had created such a terrible shortage of food supplies. People had to survive on biscuits and potato chips … and that dreadful Bihari *sattoo* (roasted chickpea flour), which Ladakhi monks may be familiar with, but no Kashmiri…."

He paused. “But now, look at this wazwan … Hafiz, how did you manage this?” Fukhtoo knew the answer but still wanted to pull Hafiz’s legs.

Hafiz looked up at the ceiling. “It’s Allah’s will, *jenab*.”

“Come on, Hafiz. Don’t bring religion into all of this. You know very well where the money has come from? Or should I tell you?” Fukhtoo could barely hide his stained yellow teeth.

“Right Sir, it’s not this Corporation’s money. It’s actually Government of India’s money for tourism promotion,” Hafiz laughed, “in any case, why should we Kashmiris pay for anything when we have access to India’s tax payers’ money? Makes no sense.”

“Watch out,” Fukhtoo warned. “PM Chiman Bhai could be keeping a close tab on you.” And let out a wheezing laughter.

Hafiz mimicked Fukhtoo’s wheezing laughter. “Not even the Prime Minister of India can micromanage us. Unless he has no other work to do.”

“Long live self-rule,” Fukhtoo said.

“Long live self-rule,” Hafiz repeated.

Fukhtoo kept his hand on Hafiz’s back. “This is what I love about Kashmir. You ask for self-rule when it suits you. And ask for Government of India’s money, when it doesn’t. A win-win situation.”

* * *

Under better circumstance, Fukhtoo would have preferred a dinner on the banks of the adjoining Dal Lake, preceded by a round of drinks. But the weather in June had already warmed up, and it was not so comfortable to hold any function, lunch, or dinner, out on SKICC lawns. Also, Islamic zealots were keeping a close watch on all anti-Islamic activities like drinking. So, one had to be careful.

Funnily the same bastards were looking forward to their 'rivers of wine' when they were dead, Fukhtoo mused. But that's how things were, and one lone Fukhtoo couldn't do much about 'modernising' Kashmiri attitudes.

Lunch over, Fukhtoo moved to Sonwar to his official residence to catch a little siesta. By the time his motorcade had crossed the boulevard and was climbing towards the Grand Hotel, he had dozed off. So, when his vehicle jerked to a stop at Gupkar in front of the CM's residence, his head hit the seat in front of him.

"What the f*** Kamal! Can't you drive properly?" Fukhtoo barked at his driver.

The driver said nothing and pointed to the barrier in front of the motorcade stopping all cars. As Fukhtoo looked out bewildered, two bulked up men in civvies approached his car. His PSO jumped out of his seat, but the men showed him their identity cards forcing the PSO to stop in his tracks. Then they knocked at Fukhtoo's window.

As he rolled down his window, the men showed their identity cards to him.

CBI (Central Bureau of Investigation) – it said in bold letters.

"Sorry Sir, you need to come with us … as we have the orders to arrest you?" One person said.

"What?" Fukhtoo was incredulous, "there must be some mistake. You know who I am, don't you?"

"Yes, Sir. You are Bashir Ahmad Fukhtoo, J&K's Chief Secretary, but we still have to take you into custody," the CBI Inspector said politely.

"And pray why?"

"Sir, do you want me to read out this whole order in public?" The Inspector pointed to Fukhtoo's motorcade staff who were all milling around his vehicle. "Or would you like to have a look at it yourself?"

Fukhtoo took the proffered piece of paper and speed read it. Beads of sweat formed on his forehead as he went through the CBI court order asking for his arrest on the grounds of exploiting a hundred and thirty-six girls sexually on the false promise of giving them government jobs, for misusing government premises (yes that included his official residence too) for performing illegal acts, for conduct "unbecoming of a government servant," and....

Meanwhile CBI Inspector number 2 had put his hand through the front seat and opened Fukhtoo's door. He indicated Fukhtoo to come out and a flustered Chief Secretary complied. CBI Inspector number 1 took out a pair of handcuffs from his back pocket. But as the onlookers watched horrified, Inspector number 2 hinted he desists, as no one expected the Chief Secretary to bolt. Instead he took Fukhtoo's left hand into his right hand indicating arrest and guided the Chief Secretary to their waiting Ambassador. Fukhtoo was bundled in the back seat of that cavernous car, and as his security watched in amazement, the Ambassador sped to the IB Guest House 200 metres ahead on the Gupkar Road where Fukhtoo's 'interrogation' was planned.

* * *

CM Ittoo was on her way to inaugurate a water supply scheme in Baramulla when her mobile rang. It was her Principal Secretary.

"Madam ... there is some horrible news."

"What?" CM Ittoo shrieked, bracing herself to hear if Delhi had dismissed her government.

"Madam, CBI has arrested the Chief Secretary and taken him to an undisclosed location."

"Huh? … Are you sure? I hope this is not one of those stupid fake news that people keep sharing on WhatsApp?"

"No, Mam. The news is confirmed. One hundred percent."

"Okay, schedule a cabinet meeting after one hour. I'm coming back right away." CM Ittoo ordered her motorcade to turn back and head for the Secretariat.

Two minutes later, she remembered something and asked her PS who was sitting with her. "Abdul, just try the PM of India."

It took about three minutes to get to the PM's office. Past the usual recordings, the PS got through to a human operator and asked to be connected to the PM. As he listened to the reply, his face fell.

"Madam, the PMO says the PM is out on a 3-day foreign tour to Europe and is currently in his aircraft. So, he can't be reached."

"Okay," CM Ittoo said, "try the Home Minister then."

This time the call went through without a hitch.

"Madam, it is the Home Minister's PA."

CM Ittoo took the mobile and said, "Halooo … PA Sahib?!" She couldn't remember the PA's name! "*Sapru Saheb hain kya*?" Is Mr Sapru in?

"Yes, Mam. Just a moment," the Home Minister's PA said as he connected the call.

"Hasinaji," Sapru said effusively, "*war-e-chhuwas?*" Is everything okay? "*Khos peth?*" Are you happy?

"Sapruji," CM Ittoo was in no mood to make polite talk in Kashmiri, "*yeh kya tamasha hai?*" What is this drama? "You arrest our Chief Secretary and don't even inform us."

Sapru was silent for a moment as if he was consulting someone. Then he said, "But Hasinaji, my office has passed on that information to your office. Didn't your Principal Secretary inform you?"

"What do you mean Sapru Saheb by 'informing me'?" Hasina was furious. "Law-and-order is a State subject and before arresting anyone in my State your agencies should have consulted us."

"Hasinaji," Sapru said in an all sugar-and-honey tone. "This is no ordinary law-and-order matter. It concerns one of our IAS (Indian Administrative Service) officers and we are fully within our rights to take whatever action we deem fit.... You sure know what this Fukhtoo fellow has done, don't you?"

CM Ittoo was silent, which meant she knew very well what her Chief Secretary was doing right under her nose. But after ages, J&K had a Kashmiri son-of-the-soil as Chief Secretary, and politically it would have been suicidal to ignore his claims to the chair of the Chief Secretary despite the fellow's sexual shenanigans.

"Hasinaji," Sapru continued. "I wish you had taken some action when young girls were being sexually exploited. But now it's too late. Let law take its own course now."

"Does the PM know?"

"Of course, he does," Sapru answered. "And he has desired that to avoid any further controversy, you should consider handing over the charge of the Chief Secretary to the next senior-most IAS officer in the cadre."

"Okay, Sapru Saheb. This is a crisis but what can we do? We are at your mercy as always! Anyway, thanks for talking to me. *Khuda Hafiz.*" Bye.

"*Khuda Hafiz*, Hasinaji." Sapru hung up.

Now who the hell is the senior-most IAS officer in J&K? CM Ittoo thought as her motorcade entered the Secretariat.

21

Srinagar, Friday, 11 June 2021 (2)

"MADAM, the cabinet is ready to meet the moment you're ready," Iqbal Qadir, the Principal Secretary to CM, said as he held the door for her.

Hasina barged in, almost pushing aside Iqbal. She went to her chair, sat down, and swivelled around. That was the indication she was really upset.

After two minutes of uncomfortable silence, she burst out, "Look at their cheek! They arrest MY Chief Secretary without even informing me. And here are we, like fools, happy with little lollipops like our separate flag, separate constitution, this stupid Article 370 which has actually not saved us from any Indian law...."

As Iqbal kept mum, CM Ittoo blabbered on for five more minutes. Suddenly she remembered, "Iqbal, do you know who the next senior-most IAS officer in the cadre is?"

"Yes, Mam. It is Raj Verma, 1987 batch, who is currently Financial Commissioner (Revenue)."

CM Ittoo went blank for a moment. "Have I met him somewhere?"

"Not recently Mam, as he doesn't sit in this Secretariat, but in the revenue complex, where the DivCom (Divisional Commissioner), Deputy Commissioner etc sit. Next to the Old Secretariat. Technically, he is the head of the revenue administration in the State and the highest court of appeal for all revenue matters in the State, below the High Court."

CM Ittoo's eyes suddenly widened in disbelief as she remembered the officer. "Isn't he … that villain of Amarnath?"

"Ur … Yes, Mam. He was the CEO of the Amarnath Shrine Board when the 2008 crisis had erupted."

"Yes … yes … now I remember. He was the one who said in a press conference that Muslim pollution was worse than Hindu pollution."

"To be fair to him, Mam," Iqbal clarified, "that's not what the government enquiry against him concluded."

CM Ittoo looked astonished. "What're you saying, Iqbal?"

"Going by the audio-video recordings of the press conference, they found he'd said something else. He'd said that it was nonsensical to claim, as some Kashmiri newspapers were claiming, that Hindu pollution was worse than Muslim pollution. And had explained what the Amarnath Shrine Board was doing to reduce pollution on the pilgrimage route –"

"Anyway, because of that fellow's communal comments, there was a total shutdown in Jammu for almost two months. The State almost split into two. And we lost elections. All thanks to the self-righteous stupidity of that Raj fellow."

Iqbal remained silent.

"But look at the cheek of the Government of India. This *batta* (a pejorative term for Kashmiri Pandits) ... Sapru, you know, who happens to be the Home Minister of India, wants me to make this same villain of Amarnath MY Chief Secretary. On my dead body ..." CM Ittoo swore.

"Any way let's go for the cabinet meeting," CM Ittoo said as she got up.

As Iqbal accompanied her, his mobile vibrated. He had a look at the number, and muttered, "Mam, this is important. I have to take this call."

As Hasina nodded absent-mindedly, Iqbal heard out the man on the other end. The call lasted for just a minute, but when Iqbal hung up, his face was ashen.

"Mam, just a minute," he whispered. "This was my batch mate at ED ... you know the Enforcement Directorate under the Ministry of Finance in Government of India?"

CM Ittoo went blank. She had heard of the IB, CBI, and R&AW, but ED? "Okay...."

"Mam, he says that the ED is acting on a tip that you have illegally obtained property at Dubai Creek Harbour of the Bin Laden Group ... as a favour to let this group start their residential projects in J&K."

"What?" CM Ittoo reeled as if someone had slapped her. Hard.

She turned back and sat on the nearest sofa in her office chambers. She tried to recall her little interaction with the Home Minister. What was he trying to convey?

Yes ... that the PM had *desired that to avoid any more controversy, you should consider handing over the charge of the Chief Secretary to the next senior-most IAS officer in the cadre.*

Did he add, Or Else?

No. Hasina was sure he didn't. Sapru was too sophisticated a person to do that openly. But this message conveyed through the ED was clear. *Do as we say. Or, be prepared to go to jail.*

CM Ittoo knew what she had to do as she got up and strode to the cabinet room.

* * *

As her cabinet colleagues got up from their chairs and stopped talking, CM Ittoo motioned them to sit and came straight to the point.

"Friends, you all know what a deep mess we have landed in, with the CBI arresting our Chief Secretary. I had taken up this matter very strongly with the Home Minister of India and would have talked to even the Indian Prime Minister but unfortunately, he was in a flight going to China." She paused not sure whether she'd said it correctly. "Or, was it Europe? Doesn't matter."

She flexed her hands. "Anyway, the Home Minister assured me that he was not taking over our powers with regard to law-and-order matters in the State. Because what our Chief Secretary did … and to tell you frankly we all knew what he was up to…. He violated the Conduct Rules of the All-India Services, where Government of India has full jurisdiction.

"So, we are literally at the receiving end … till we have these All-India Service officers serving us. But *Insha'Allah*, that day is not far when we will snatch our independence and shall be free from all such stupid Indian rules and laws that shackle us."

"*Insha'Allah*," all Cabinet Ministers exclaimed in unison as they thumped their tables enthusiastically.

"But right now," CM Ittoo continued, "our topmost priority is to appoint a new Chief Secretary. And the five officers who could be in the zone of consideration are … Raj

Verma, who is FC(R) ..." CM Ittoo paused and cocked her head towards Iqbal. "Iqbal, who are the other four?"

So, Iqbal mentioned the name of the three officers who were in Delhi serving the Government of India, and the fifth who was in J&K.

"Hasinaji," Graboo said who was the Finance Minister, "we can't go by seniority here because the senior-most is just not fit to hold this sensitive assignment. We all know about the intemperate comments he made during the Amarnath crisis. So many lives were lost then, all because of that utterly communal and irresponsible fellow – Raj Verma."

"Yes Hasinaji," the Agriculture Minister piped in, "I suggest we try to get the next senior-most from Delhi. But my vote is also against this villain of Amarnath."

"The Delhi-wallas are generally reluctant to cut short their tenure and come back to the State," Hansraj, the Rural Development Minister from Jammu, said. "So why not give Banarsi Das Gandotra, our own Jammu boy a chance? Unlike Raj Verma, he's a local. He's currently the Planning Commissioner, so he has a good grip over all departments of the State. We all know how polite and accommodating he is with respect to all our demands. On the other hand, we all know how arrogant this Raj Verma is. Why, only last week I was pleading with him not to transfer a *patwari* from my constituency, but he was adamant that the *patwari* had completed his tenure and had to go. And he went ahead and transferred him. I have never felt so humiliated."

"Hansrajji," CM Ittoo intervened, "we appreciate your sentiments. But your boy Gandotra is not even in the Chief Secretary's grade. So first we have to promote him to that grade and then make him Chief Secretary. Also, officially what do we say against this Raj Verma? About superseding him by an officer five year his junior? There could be legal implications...."

Other ministers jumped in the fray. There were heated discussions, in favour of every candidate, except Raj Verma. Since there were no Kashmiri Muslim officers in the list, the majority were tilting in favour of the other local boy, even if he belonged to Jammu. CM Ittoo had to intervene now.

"Friends, this is indeed a very difficult decision for us to take. That's why I wanted to consult the Indian PM but couldn't. But the message I got back from the Home Minister was clear. The PM wants us to hand over the charge of the Chief Secretary to the next senior-most IAS officer in the cadre. To help avoid any controversy. Mind you, they're not dictating to us, which in any case I will not allow till I'm alive. But they are asking us to *consider* the senior-most. So, just to avoid any further controversy, as the Indian PM says, I think it prudent to give the charge of Chief Secretary to this Raj Verma. But this shall be a totally temporary arrangement till we sort out all the technical hitches. Okay?"

There were still some murmurs of protest. CM Ittoo let silence return to the room. Then she turned towards the Commissioner/Secretary General Administration (GAD) Department and said, "Kakru, you heard us. Please get my approval to issue the orders right away."

She turned towards her Principal Secretary. "And Iqbal, call the new Chief Secretary for a meeting immediately."

22

Srinagar, Friday, 11 June 2021 (3)

RAJ was busy giving finishing touches to his order on the latest revenue court case when his office was flooded with people. First to land in were all the 'anti-national-pro-Kashmiri-freedom-Pakistan-loving' lawyers who always had their antennas in the right places. Next was the staff of the FC(R)'s office, who were tipped off by the clerks in the GAD office who were typing and 'dispatching' the order appointing Raj as Chief Secretary.

"*Mubarakan* ... *Mubarakan* ... we knew the brilliance of our worthy FC(R) would be recognised soon," a gushing lawyer said as he grabbed the right hand of Raj and shook it vigorously.

"What's it Khan Saheb?" Raj was surprised.

"Come on *Jenab*, don't be so coy. Don't you know you are the new Chief Secretary?" another lawyer piped in.

Just then the phone rang. It was the Principal Secretary to CM on the other side, confirming the news and also conveying that Madam CM wanted to see Raj right away.

"Okay Iqbal. But shouldn't you give me a copy of the order first?" Raj said.

"No problem, Sir. I'm faxing it right away."

In a minute, the LaserJet-cum-fax machine in Raj's office room was whirring as it spat out a government order. It had the usual number and date of a GAD order, but the body sounded 'funny'. It read:

In the interest of administration, it is hereby ordered that till further orders the charge of the post of Chief Secretary shall be ***temporarily*** *held by Shri Raj Verma (IAS '87) Financial Commissioner (Revenue) in addition to his own duties.*

By order of the Government of Jammu and Kashmir.

Commissioner/Secretary to Government, General Administration Department

Signed

Raj sighed as he read the order. He held up the order and said, "Okay, friends. There is nothing to be euphoric about. I have the order here and it says that I just have to keep the Chief Secretary's seat warm till Bashir comes back from his little picnic."

A collective sigh escaped the lips of those gathered around Raj as he collected his papers and moved out to visit the CM.

Five minutes later Raj was in the visitor's room next to the CM's office on the 3rd floor of the Civil Secretariat Srinagar. Iqbal rushed in and requested him to come to his office as that was a little bigger and more exclusive. Raj complied reluctantly.

Five minutes passed by. Then 10. Raj looked at his watch. So, he's being shown his place, he sighed.

Iqbal sensing Raj's discomfort got up to check what the holdup was. As he suspected, there were no visitors with the CM. So, he peeped in to announce that the new Chief Secretary had come to call on the CM.

CM Ittoo looked up at the wall clock and decided it was time she let the Chief Secretary come in. Iqbal rushed back and escorted Raj to CM's office chambers.

"Congratulations Verma Saheb, how are you?" CM Ittoo said with a smile.

"Thank you, Madam. I'm okay. I just wanted to say that it's really very kind of you all to consider me for this assignment."

"Oh ... yes ... yes, please sit down. And Iqbal, can you send us some tea please? Or would you prefer some coffee, Raj Saheb?"

Raj was taken aback at the unusual courtesy being shown to him.

"Whatever you prefer, Mam," he mumbled.

"A strong cup of coffee then," CM Ittoo said as she dismissed Iqbal.

There was some uncomfortable silence till the coffee arrived. Then CM Ittoo asked, "Verma Saheb, I hope you are happy with this assignment."

"Mam, my happiness is immaterial. Since the government has asked me to hold this additional charge, for the time being, I'll just do that to the best of my abilities."

"Additional charge? What do you mean?" CM Ittoo blinked.

"Mam, the order asks me *to hold* the charge of the post of Chief Secretary, in addition to my own duties, *temporarily*, till further orders, which means I have to continue my work as

FC(R) and dispose of the additional work of the Chief Secretary whenever such papers are brought to me. It also means that as per convention I shouldn't sit in the chair of the Chief Secretary, and instead continue to operate from my current office, continue to draw my pay against the post of FC(R), and so on … just as additional charges are handled when some officer goes on leave?"

There was a moment's silence, where after CM Ittoo exploded. "This is the best I could do, and you are quoting some official mumbo-jumbo and displaying your ungratefulness? To me? Do you know how much you had damaged your reputation by uttering those insensitive remarks against Muslims when you were heading that godforsaken Amarnath Shrine Board? Do you know how much I had to fight against my own cabinet colleagues to get this so-called additional charge handed over to you? Do you know what they all call you? The Villain of Amarnath … But if you still don't want to come to the Secretariat, or sit in the Chief Secretary's chair, it is your funeral. I've no views in the matter."

Raj remained silent. CM Ittoo said nothing that he didn't know. Also, she was willing to do nothing to redress the 'technical problems' mentioned by him. So fine, as an obedient government servant, he'd carry out the orders, exactly as they were worded.

There was another moment of uncomfortable silence as CM Ittoo glared at Raj.

He got up from his chair. "Is there anything else you desire, Madam?"

CM Ittoo kept glaring.

"Then, Good Day Madam." Raj said as he got out of the CM's office.

* * *

CM Ittoo was aghast at the cheek. *What does this mole of Government of India want?* She'd soon teach him, and his master Sapru, a lesson they'd never forget.

The moment the doors closed behind Raj Verma, she picked up her mobile and dialled an unlisted number. The call was immediately picked up.

"Yes, Mam."

"Abu Bhai, this time it will have to be Raj Verma, our new Chief Secretary."

"Did you say Chief Secretary?"

"Yes."

"Then the time and place will have to be of our own choosing."

"So be it," CM Ittoo said as she disconnected the call.

23

Srinagar, Friday, 11 June 2021 (4)

THE Secretariat staff almost mobbed Raj as he came out of the CM's office. Prominent among them were the staff of the Chief Secretary who wanted to escort Raj to that hallowed room. Raj refused saying he had no time and took to the stairs.

"But Sir," Nawal, the PPS (Principal Personal Secretary) of the Chief Secretary, said, "there are some files to be cleared."

"What files?" Raj queried as he continued climbing down to get to his car.

"Sir, granting casual leave to Secretary-level officers, sanctioning their official trips to Delhi, and so on."

"Ah, you can always send such routine files to my office, and I'll clear them from there." Raj reached the ground floor.

Nawal huffed-and-puffed to reach Raj's car to open the door for him, which he acknowledged with a nod and got in. Five minutes later, Raj was back in his old office. The crowd of well-wishers had disappeared, but they'd be back soon, Raj sighed.

As he sat down to resume his work on the revenue order he was working on, his phone buzzed. It was his PA, in a super-excited tone, "Sir, it is the Cabinet Secretary. From Delhi."

As Raj pressed the button to take the call, the voice on the other end said, "Just a moment, Sir."

There was a click and a buzz and the familiar voice could be heard immediately. "Raj, this is Sanjeev."

"Good afternoon, Sir."

"My office has been trying to reach you for quite some time but apparently you never went to the Chief Secretary's office. So, tell me, why are you still sitting in your own office? What happened? Haven't the orders been issued?"

So, Raj gave a long explanation about how the Chief Secretary's charge was given to him 'temporarily', and 'in addition to his own duties', and how it was against the tradition of the civil service to occupy the higher chair under such conditions, and so on.

"Ah, so they are still playing games!" The Cabinet Secretary was incredulous. "Doesn't matter. Raj, can you fax me a copy of this order?" The steeliness in the voice at the other end was disconcerting.

"Right away Sir." And as the call disconnected, Raj got his PA to fax the order.

24

Srinagar, Sunday, 13 June 2021 (1)

ANOTHER day passed by. Routine files from the Chief Secretary's office kept landing on Raj's desk in the office of the FC(R), and Raj kept on 'disposing' them off.

Sunday came. Raj was readying himself for his weekly round of golf in the Police Golf Course, which allowed a cheaper six-monthly membership, than the super-exclusive and super-expensive Royal Springs Golf Course, when he got a call from the CM's office about an emergency cabinet meeting at Dachigam Guest House at 1100 hrs. And CM Ittoo desired that Raj reach about half-an-hour early.

Raj called his driver and PSO to come by 0945, who in turn alerted the Chief Secretary's security. And so, when Raj came out at 1000 hrs, the entire motorcade of the Chief Secretary with two cars in front and one behind was ready to whisk him to Dachigam. Raj was flabbergasted, but there was no time to create a fuss.

At 1001, the motorcade was off, going down the Raj Bhavan Road from Cheshmeshahi. In two minutes, it had hit the Boulevard with the sprawling Dal Lake on its left. This was the cleanest portion of the Dal, and Raj had to admit that the lake looked absolutely 'awesome' at this point.

Five minutes later, the famed Mughal garden Nishat was on the right side, its stout walls delineating its temporary status as a fortified structure from the time the great Mughals used to camp here with their *harem*. But the Dal Lake on the left was now full of green algae and weeds. There were boatmen on *shikaras* valiantly taking them out. But Raj knew that was a drama only to please the courts. If the Honourable courts were serious, they should have gone straight to the source of the pollution – the untreated sewers going into the lake from houseboats and hotels. But that would be too much, politically! That's why one had to endure this drama of taking out the weeds manually, Raj sighed.

Soon they were going past Shalimar, another famous Mughal garden. This was where the famous conductor Zubin Mehta had once performed in September 2013. That looked like ancient history because now no one could even dream of such a musical soiree in this jihadi-infested valley.

Raj's motorcade approached Harwan, the third and the smallest Mughal garden in Srinagar. Raj looked out on his right to check the water level in the adjacent lake above the garden and was happy that it was filled to the brim. And yes, those nasty Dal Lake weeds had still not reached its crystal blue waters.

At the first sight of the motorcade, the gates of the Dachigam Wild Life Sanctuary, normally barred for common folks, flung open with an alacrity that amused Raj. Temporary charge or not, at least the guards here were treating him like a full-fledged Chief Secretary. The gurgling Dachigam River was enchanting as usual, and Raj thought he saw a silver trout jump out of the waters and fall back.

The Government Trout farm passed by on the right as the motorcade sped past to the State Guest House. Soon they were inside its picturesque compound.

As Raj got out, the Guest House attendant informed him that they expected Madam CM any moment. But two Cabinet Ministers were already sitting on the lawns.

Raj thought it prudent to say hello and sauntered towards the old walnut trees under whose shade the ministers were sitting. The ministers got up on seeing Raj. One shook hands warmly congratulating him on 'this well-deserved promotion'. Another took Raj in an effusive bear hug as if he were a long-lost friend!

Then they all sat down as liveried waiters from the State Government's Hospitality and Protocol Department scurried around serving them tea and cashew nuts.

It was almost 11 and there was still no sign of the CM. Suddenly, the mobiles of both ministers buzzed. As they took the call, Raj could see their faces fall. Both got up and rushed out saying there was an emergency they had to attend.

And the cabinet meeting be damned, Raj wondered.

Now Raj was the only senior person left around the sprawling complex. He asked his PSO to check-up, but he got no news about the impending arrival of the CM or any other Cabinet Minister.

Raj got up and moved towards the Guest House building. Every time he came to Dachigam, he couldn't help marvel at its magnificent facade that was tiled with hundreds of square feet of real walnut tree bark. That gave it such a quaint tree-house kind of look that made it the favourite guest house of so many Indian Prime Ministers and Presidents from Mrs Indira Gandhi onwards.

Raj wanted to have a look inside to check if anything had changed since his last visit to this property and opened the door of the VVIP room.

"Welcome Chief Secretary Saheb," a gruff voice said from the inside.

As Raj stepped in and squinted to find who it was, he recoiled in horror. There were five bearded men wearing *pherans* and holding an AK-47 each in their hands. The VVIP room was actually brimming with hard core terrorists!

As he involuntarily tried to step out, the voice said, "I won't do that if I were you. Sit down. Please."

The voice was in heavily accented Punjabi, and it was not polite at all. That must be a Pakistani terrorist then.

The chiselled bearded face and the sharp nose caught Raj's attention. And he wondered why the face looked so familiar.

25

Srinagar, Sunday, 13 June 2021 (2)

STUNNED, Raj sat down on the nearest sofa. His mind whirred with scenarios. The audacity of these terrorists, that they were trying to abduct J&K's Chief Secretary from the most secure guest house in the Valley, overwhelmed him.

They made last such attempt some 20 years back when Mr Mehmood-ur-Rehman (1966 IAS JK) as J&K's Home Secretary had visited Dachigam. The year was 2001. Terrorists had surrounded the place but word got out and the army flew in their choppers to rescue Mr Rehman. Just in time.

Before that on 8 December 1989, JKLF (J&K Liberation Front) had abducted Rubaiya Sayeed, daughter of the then-Home Minister of India Mufti Mohammad Sayeed and kept her in a house in the Dachigam area. She was released some 122 hours later when the government agreed to release five dreaded terrorists in exchange.

Raj remembered how then there was no sympathy for poor Rubaiya. And he suspected same would be the reaction in Kashmir when the news of his abduction got out.

Rubaiya episode was considered a watershed moment in Kashmir. As a journalist reported, "Till then everyone was treating militancy as a joke. People used to say, *hey, my cousin has become a militant, he has a gun now....*"

When those terrorists were freed, there was all around jubilation. Kashmiris sang, danced, and raised anti-India slogans.

"*Jo kare khuda se khauf, wo uthale Kalashnikov* (If you fear god, pick up an AK-47 gun)," was one, in addition to the usual, "Indian dogs go back," "*Jeeve jeeve Pakistan* (May Pakistan continue to live)," "*Hum kya chahe Azaadi* (What we want is freedom)" and so on.

"Nothing short of a blunder," Dr Farooq Abdullah, the then Chief Minister had retorted when asked about his views on the release. According to him, JKLF was just bluffing, and they would have never harmed Rubaiya.

But Raj knew that in his case these Pakistani terrorists were NOT bluffing. He didn't yet know what they wanted, but he remembered how that Rubaiya's episode had emboldened the secessionists and pro-Pakistan elements. People saw India brought to her knees for the first time. It made them feel that *azaadi* (independence) was only a short distance away.

Raj hated the prospect of that story repeated all-over again.

Suddenly he remembered his PSO and asked, "Where is my staff?"

"Sleeping," the bearded Pakistani said with a grin that was disconcerting.

Seeing the alarm on Raj's face, the terrorist guffawed, "Oh, don't worry. They're not dead. We just served them our special tea and they all are happily snoozing."

"And the guards at the gate?"

"Same treatment. They also love to eat, and so they are daydreaming peacefully. With their hands and feet tied, of course."

Oh my God! That's a brazen violation of all SOPs (Standard Operating Procedure) that forbade eating together for all security staff. But trust these Kashmiris not to trust any SOPs, Raj thought.

"By the way, I'm Abu Farzana. From the Lashkar-e-Toiba."

Abu Farzana? The Commander of Lashkar-e-Toiba? The name rang a bell. He was THE wanted-dead-or-alive kind of terrorist. Raj had seen his name and pictures on television and newspapers a couple of times. No wonder his face looked so familiar.

"And here are my Kashmiri *wafadaars* (faithful) Mustafa, Shaukat, Aziz, and Ahmad," the lead terrorist introduced his team in a tone reserved for introducing your pet dogs.

"Abu Farzana, from Muridke? Why didn't you say that before?" Raj said in chaste Punjabi.

Abu was taken aback, and asked back in Punjabi, "Why, have you been to Muridke?"

"Been? What are you saying? My whole family migrated to India from Muridke in 1947." Raj continued in Punjabi.

Abu was puzzled. "From which colony did your family migrate?"

"Hey, I wasn't even born then. So how do I know? But I only remember my grandmother talking of the lovely mustard field, and the village pond, and …" Raj continued with his generalised description of a typical Punjabi village.

"Abu Bhai," said Mustafa, the Kashmiri lad, "how does it matter where this *kafir* (infidel) came from? Tell me when we bump him off?"

"Bump him off? Are you mad? Thank God, *Peer Saheb* has made me in-charge of this mission." Raj was surprised at the sharpness in Abu's voice that made the Kashmiri cringe. Raj also realised how Abu was throwing around the name of Syed Salahuddin, the Pakistan-based terrorist leader of Hizbul Mujahedeen, who was respectfully addressed as *Peer Saheb*.

"And Chief Secretary Saheb, don't worry. Even if you were not from Muridke, I'd have looked after you well. You are a *sone ki murgi* (a golden goose) for us, after all."

A golden goose? That was alarming. Raj had to know a little more.

"Abu Bhai, don't you think you have taken a huge risk by coming to Dachigam when our entire cabinet, along with the CM, is about to descend with hundreds of security personnel?"

Abu again guffawed and this time those four Kashmiris too joined in the fun.

"Chief Secretary Saheb, who told you the cabinet is coming here today? Are you really that stupid, despite being my village bum, sorry, brother?"

Blood drained from Raj's face. Okay, so there was never any plan to hold a cabinet meeting in Dachigam today. Even the two ministers who had landed earlier (by mistake?) scurried away the moment they were told of the terrorists' plan.

And the CM? Looks like she too had no intention of coming here today. So, was she also a party to the plan of abducting him? 'The villain of Amarnath' as she was never tired of rubbing it in?

Everything suddenly made sense.

Raj shook his head in disbelief, and asked, "Okay, Abu. I get the idea. But what's the game plan now?"

Abu smiled, and said, "Why don't we watch some TV?"

And he used the remote to switch on the telly.

The TV was tuned to play the Pakistani channel Geo TV first. Despite government orders that no Pakistani channels be played in India, Raj sighed.

An excited female anchor was narrating BREAKING NEWS.

"The Chief Secretary of the Indian held Kashmir was captured without firing a single shot by Hizbul Mujahedeen today at 1030 hrs in Srinagar. It is learnt that the holy warriors, in exchange, have demanded the release of five innocent Pakistanis that are rotting in Indian jails for the last so many years."

Abu changed the channel to an Indian TV station. The same news again. Except, that this one was also displaying file photos of the 'innocent Pakistanis' that were sought to be released. And, of course, they were all hard-core *jihadi* terrorists.

Raj noted that all channels were claiming that he was abducted around 1030 hrs when he had not even reached Dachigam by that time. Did it mean that his capture was a foregone conclusion regardless of when the actual event took place?

Suddenly, a loudspeaker from a nearby mosque blared the *azaan*, the Muslim call for prayers.

"Mustafa, you keep an eye on our worthy Chief Secretary, as we finish our prayers." Abu Farzana ordered as he marched out to the attached bedroom of the VVIP suite with his three Kashmiri compatriots.

26

Srinagar, Sunday, 13 June 2021 (3)

THE loudspeaker of the nearest mosque crackled to life. Again. But this time this was no *azaan*.

Instead a commanding voice boomed in Urdu:

"Abu Farzana, *tumko charo taraf se gher liya gaya hai. Hath utha kar bahar aa jao, ya marne ke liye taiyar ho jao."* You are surrounded from all sides. Come out with your hands held high or be prepared to be die.

Ah, so the army has arrived. Raj heaved a sigh of relief.

That was a bit premature, because the same message was now repeated in Kashmiri. To set all doubts at rest, the Kashmiri voice now even introduced himself as IG Kashmir Mushtaq Bhat.

That's why Farzana was continuing with his prayers, confident that the announcements were, er ... just announcements. Or, because he knew that the local police were under instructions NOT to disturb the great Abu Farzana?

But ... But ... But ... what about rescuing the State's Chief Secretary? Didn't his abduction warrant intervention at the highest level of the armed forces?

For an outsider like him? Raj sighed. As a 'non-State subject', 'outsider' All-India Service officer, whose plight Madam Monali Kumar had highlighted so well in her epochal work *The Outsider's Curse*, Raj knew that he too suffered from a 'curse'. A curse that ensured that unlike any other State, in J&K, he couldn't buy property, couldn't educate his children in any medical or engineering college, couldn't get his spouse or children to find employment with the State government, could neither vote in nor stand for any State-level elections even after retirement, couldn't even get his son married to a local girl because that will immediately extinguish that girl's State-subjectship....

So why should the State Government bother to requisition the army to save his life? Suddenly, it all made so much sense.

Just then, Farzana came out with his three colleagues. He asked the person guarding Raj till then to go offer his prayers.

Raj couldn't help but notice the ear-to-ear smile plastered on Farzana's face.

As he thought of asking Farzana the reason, Farzana guffawed, "Chief Secretary Saheb, *yeh Mushtaq to apna banda hai.*" This IG Mushtaq fellow is our man. "So, don't worry. No one will disturb you from enjoying our hospitality."

Raj panicked. His stomach knotted.

"Farzana Bhai, you know as an outsider non-State subject officer, my life has no value. So, I think you are just wasting your time waiting for the government to release your colleagues...."

"Shut up Chief Secretary Saheb. And don't spoil my mood," Farzana snarled. The ferocity of his voice stunned Raj.

"Ah, don't let me be nasty to my village brother. So why don't we watch some TV?" Funnily, Farzana was soft again.

And once again the TV was switched on.

Farzana flicked through few news channels, but it looked like Raj's abduction was now stale news. They were all now focusing on some train accident near Agra.

Farzana then switched to a Hindi Bollywood songs channel and started dancing. He ignored the look of horror on his colleagues' face for such an anti-Islamic act.

* * *

The Prime Minister had just boarded his special plane at Charles de Gaulle Airport, Paris on his way to India when his Private Secretary rushed in. "It's the NSA Sir."

The PM took the call. His face fell as the National Security Advisor briefed him on the full sequence of events leading to the abduction of J&K's Chief Secretary. The call lasted hardly two minutes with the PM listening intently. The pilots waited till he finished the call, lest it be disconnected during take-off.

"Sir, it's time to launch Operation Revenge," the NSA concluded.

"I agree," the PM nodded as he signalled his staff to let the aircraft commence its take-off schedule.

* * *

Naseem Geelani, the youngest son of Syed Ali Shah Geelani the octogenarian separatist leader, was returning home after a gruelling session with the NIA (National Investigation Agency) about the Pakistani currency found in his possession. Some Gujjars with their sheep and goats were walking ahead probably to the meadows of Gulmarg. That had created a traffic jam, with cars and two wheelers honking and madly weaving around the sheep.

Naseem was irritated as hell. So, when he heard a knock on his car window, he thought it would be a beggar who he will have to abuse to shoo him away.

The sight of the gun instead froze him. The gunman motioned him to come out which Naseem did. Suddenly three more men emerged from the shadows. One got into Naseem's car as if the car belonged to him. The other two escorted Naseem to the adjacent narrow side street to a van marked AMBULANCE which whisked all of them away.

* * *

46-year-old Shahid Yousuf had just sat down for dinner. It was the usual Kashmiri fare. Mutton *Roganjosh*, the red-coloured mutton curry, boiled rice, and *Karam saag* (Collard Greens). Like most Kashmiris, Shahid could eat this stuff every day and not get bored.

Unlike other Kashmiris, however, Shahid was never worried about his security. Being the son of Syed Salahuddin, the Chief of the dreaded terrorist organisation Hizbul Mujahedeen, obviously had its own perks.

Instead of being stigmatised, his father's reputation had in fact got Yousuf a master's degree in agriculture and a job as a village agricultural assistant in the State Government's agriculture department. He didn't have to go to office, of course, and his monthly salary from the government was disbursed to him at his residence on the first of every month without fail. That left Shahid free to focus on managing the vast financial and real estate assets of his terrorist father, full-time.

Like most Kashmiri houses, Shahid's main doors were never latched till the time they were awake. So, it was not a strange sight to find three men suddenly walking through without even so much of a "May we come in?"

A look at their burly frames, and the mean look in their eyes, and Shahid knew these were no ordinary Kashmiris who had come to pay their 'tributes' to his great father.

"Agency guys," Shahid muttered as he got up from his dinner table.

One person indicated the sink to Shahid to let him wash his hands. The other two had by then taken out their AK-47s.

As Shahid's wife stifled a scream, the three strangers had escorted Shahid out of the main door to their jeep and had disappeared.

* * *

There were two more abductions that night. One involved Maryam, the 13-year-old daughter of Mirwaiz Umar Farooq, a prominent Hurriyat leader of Kashmir. The other person was Raziyah Sultana, the 10-year-old daughter of Yasin Malik, the Chairman of J&K Liberation Front.

Surprisingly, there were no demands for ransom. No rival terrorist group tried to claim credit for the abductions either. Although all four families tried to file reports with the police, their complaints were not recorded 'on orders from above'.

There was a total black out on TV and radio too. That suited the four separatist families as their invincible reputation in the Valley otherwise would have been in serious jeopardy.

* * *

The police barricading the Dachigam State Guest House had very thoughtfully sent in some food for their Chief Secretary. And, of course, the terrorists.

Typical Kashmiri fare, with Kashmiri boiled rice, *yakhni* (a yoghurt-based mutton curry), mutton kebabs, cauliflower, and

Rajma. The guest house being next to the biggest trout hatchery in India, the platter had five deep-fried trout pieces too.

The terrorists were salivating, but Farzana was suspicious. What if they had laced the food with drugs? After all, on a mission the rule was that they survive only on 'dry fruits' like almonds and raisins.

"Let this *Kafir* taste it first," Farzana barked pushing the plate towards Raj.

It was almost 2 PM and Raj was as hungry as anyone else. So, he happily grabbed the plate and served himself a little from each dish.

Farzana watched him eat the fish and then the mutton, and remarked, "Hey look, this Hindu doesn't just eat *ghaas-phoos* (grass etc)."

Raj didn't react and kept on eating.

"And here are we thinking that one Muslim soldier is equal to ten Hindus because we eat meat," Farzana chuckled.

Raj didn't want to contradict Farzana about the robust non-vegetarian tradition in all corners of India. So, he quietly served himself some more rice, and put some *yakhni* curry on top of that.

Farzana looked at his colleagues and decided enough was enough.

"Okay, I don't think the police would try to drug their Chief Secretary. So, let's also eat."

That was the signal the terrorists were waiting for. They all sat down around the vessels and started serving themselves.

Raj was surprised that even the guard who was supposed to be on the lookout had joined in.

They must be absolutely certain that NO police action is going to take place while they have lunch, he mused.

Farzana was into his second helping when his phone rang.

What timing?! He cursed under his breath. But he took the call as it was on the satellite phone.

Farzana's face fell. He kept on saying, "Yes, *Peer Saheb* … as you say … your wish is my command…."

"*Peer Saheb*?" Raj's head reeled in alarm. That would be Syed Salahuddin himself, the ruthless Pakistan-based Kashmiri chief of the dreaded Hizbul Mujahedeen.

Raj knew the story well – of how an ordinary political worker Mohammad Yousuf had evolved into the infamous Syed Salahuddin. How he was arrested by the police for campaigning against the National Conference, the ruling party, in 1987, how he was beaten up by a National Conference Cabinet Minister while in police custody, how the National Conference then used government machinery to stuff ballot boxes in their favour, and how as a result the National Conference managed to come back to power in J&K with a thumping majority.

"I'll manage that, *Peer Saheb*, don't worry," Farzana assured the voice on the other end as he disconnected the call.

Raj had a nasty feeling about this conversation. Was Salahuddin asking Farzana to execute him?

Raj had suddenly lost his appetite. So, he got up and indicated to his soiled hand. "Farzana Bhai, if you permit, I'll just wash up."

As Farzana nodded absent-mindedly, Raj moved to the bedroom, and to its attached toilet. Surprisingly, Farzana asked no one to follow Raj.

So, Raj used the soap kept on the sink to lather and clean his hands. While doing that, he stole a glance at the bathroom window, which was latched all right but like almost all windows in Kashmir, had no grills.

As no one was keeping an eye on him, Raj latched the bathroom door from inside and quickly opened the bathroom window. He winced involuntarily as the window creaked. But as there was no reaction from anywhere, he hoisted himself on the window sill and got out.

The creak alerted the terrorists. "I think this Chief Secretary bastard is trying to escape." One of Farzana's men got up.

Farzana motioned him to sit down and sighed, "Sorry guys, today is not the day for your martyrdom. The *kafirs* have been too smart. We arrested one Chief Secretary, but they abducted four. And you know who? Peer Saheb and Geelani Saheb's sons, and the daughters of Mirwaiz and Yousuf Malik. *Ya Khuda, kitne zalim hai yeh log."* O God, how ruthless are these people?

Seeing the shell-shocked faces of his colleagues, Farzana guffawed, "Now don't be so morose. What if we lost a small battle? There is a bigger war ahead that I'm sure we'll win."

"*Insha'Allah*," every one said as they followed Farzana to the main door and sauntered on upstream of the Dachigam River.

No one will dare stop them or chase them – this Farzana was certain.

* * *

Raj was crouching and running. Stumbling and crawling. Any moment he expected to hear a shout and a shot from the Guest House side.

Suddenly, he heard a shout from the direction he was heading. A shot whizzed above him. Raj went plonk on the ground and stayed there till he was surrounded by excited police men. Raj was surprised that they had recognised him despite his mud-plastered face and dishevelled condition.

Soon wireless sets crackled informing the police top brass about the dramatic rescue of the State Chief Secretary.

By the time Raj reached home, the TV channels were full of Raj's heroic act in escaping from the clutches of the deadly Farzana gang. Soon his little lawn was swarming with staff from his office.

CM Ittoo announced an award and sent in a message that she wanted to confer the award personally on Raj, but he ignored that.

The second message was from the Prime Minister.

And Raj caught the last flight out of Srinagar to go to Delhi.

27

Delhi, Sunday, 13 June 2021

THE IndiGo flight from Srinagar took the usual one hour forty minutes to reach Delhi but some flight congestion at the Indira Gandhi International Airport delayed the flight by about twenty minutes. By the time, Raj got out of the airport terminal 2, it was almost 8 PM.

The traffic in Delhi on a Monday evening was creepy-crawly as usual. So, Raj spent an hour more before he could reach his government accommodation in New Moti Bagh, Chanakyapuri. He longed to meet Sangeeta and his son.

When Raj reached his apartment, the place looked like nothing he had ever seen. A crowd had gathered outside his house – OB vans from almost all prominent TV news channels, curious neighbours, excited stray dogs, and men in *Khakis* trying to impose some order. The moment he got down from his J&K House's official vehicle, the entire crowd seemed to pounce upon him shoving mikes in his face.

"Mr Verma, how do you feel after escaping from the terrorists?"

"Raj Saheb, what was the secret deal after which the terrorists let you go?"

"Were any terrorists killed in the rescue operation?"

"Who do you think masterminded this abduction?"

"Do you think some politicians too were involved?"

Before Raj could think of answering one question, another mike was thrust into his face with another question. The barrage of questions fogged up his brain. He wanted to shout, abuse, and thrash a few reporters, but a lifetime spent in the IAS forced him to keep his cool.

"Look guys," Raj climbed up the bonnet of a van to reach some higher ground, "I'm grateful for all your interest in my well-being. But at the moment, I don't have answers to most of your questions. So please hold on for some time till the JK Police concludes its investigations. I would love to meet you some other time. But it was a long day today and if you'll excuse me, I'll just try to get some rest."

The reporters protested, "Just one question, Sir."

But Raj bounded up the stairs to reach his flat on the first floor.

* * *

Monday, June 14, 2021 Delhi

Raj had to meet the Prime Minister at 1130 the next day in *Vigyan Bhavan* (literally Science House) where the PM was scheduled to inaugurate the annual day functions of FICCI (Federation of Indian Industry and Commerce).

As Raj reached the prestigious convention centre on the Maulana Azad Road in Central Delhi by 1100 hrs he couldn't help admiring the grandeur of the entire complex. He couldn't believe that this edifice built way back in 1956 was designed not by some legendary foreign architect but by RL Gehlote of the humble Central Public Works Department (CPWD) of the Government of India. The CPWD was famous for designing buildings with terrible flaws – poor workmanship, bad plumbing, paint that falls off with time, seepage, and so on. Nothing to be proud of.

But this building was a marvel – a mish-mash of elements of the British Raj structures, along with Hindu, Mughal, and ancient Buddhist architecture, especially the Chaitya arches of Ajanta Caves. But why was it called 'Science House', Raj had no clue.

The SPG (Special Protection Group), that guards the PM, screened his credentials and escorted him to the VVIP lounge. There were some newspapers neatly arranged on the centre table. Raj picked up the *Economic Times* and sat down on a leather sofa. His eyes fell on the half-page colour advertisement announcing proudly the PM's address to FICCI.

Raj stared at the wall clock. It was almost 1125 hrs when he heard a loud round of applause from the Plenary Hall, the hall where the PM was delivering a speech. That meant that the speech was over. Raj almost got up from the sofa but the SPG commando smiled and indicated with his eyes to keep sitting.

It was almost 10 minutes before the PM could make his grand entry into the VVIP lounge. Raj got up with alacrity. As the SPG commandoes barred the entry of common people into the lounge, Raj introduced himself but the PM cut him short.

"Ah, don't bother. The whole country knows you by now."

Raj was dumbstruck.

"So Rajji, tell me what really happened?" the PM asked as he sat down on his sofa.

Raj started from the beginning. The notice of the cabinet meeting in Dachigam on a Sunday. The two ministers in Dachigam who at the earliest opportunity scooted. His 'abduction' and his interactions with the dreaded Abu Farzana. His dramatic escape, which in hindsight he thought was all staged.

The PM appeared to hear intently, but Raj suspected he knew most of his story already. The PM buzzed for his attendant and looking to Raj asked, "Some tea? Or coffee?"

Raj struggled to reply as it was most unusual for an Indian PM to offer tea to a lowly bureaucrat.

"Ah, I need a strong cup of coffee very badly. Please get two cups ... or make it three as Sartaj Saheb should be joining us any moment," the PM asked the attendant who was waiting for the orders.

Sartaj? Would that be Sartaj Daniel, the cloak-and-dagger NSA?

Just then, there was a knock, and the burly NSA made a grand entry. Raj again got up and introduced himself. The NSA shook hands firmly with him, almost making Raj wince in pain.

"Nice to know you are alive and kicking, young man," Daniel said. "So Raj," Daniel had now taken the lead, "who do you think was responsible for your abduction?"

"Sir, the Pakistanis as always. The terrorist leading the operation was a fellow from Muridke who I had to humour pretending I too was from his village."

"That was some quick thinking. But what about those two ministers, who you met in the Guest House, and who chose to escape minutes before they caught you?"

"Sir, they definitely were tipped off but I'm not sure if they were a party…." Raj said hesitatingly.

"And your CM? Was she a party or was she too similarly tipped off?" Daniel's gaze was now boring into Raj's eyes.

Raj was too stunned to react. Sure, CM Ittoo never wanted an outsider like him to be the Chief Secretary. Sure, Raj had pondered about the possibility of the CM being in the know of the operation. But to think of her masterminding it all was preposterous *prima facie* as his lawyer friends would have declared in his FC(R)'s court. All said and done, Raj thought, Kashmiris were not so *ehsaan faramosh* (ungrateful) as to get one of their senior most bureaucrats abducted or bumped of.

"Okay," Daniel said, "so let me tell you the inside story. My Pakistani sources tell me that the demand for abducting you came directly from the CM."

Raj felt like the rug had been pulled underneath his feet and he almost tumbled backwards. Almost.

"But why Sir?" he stammered. Raj had no reason to disbelieve Daniel, who as everyone knew had formidable contacts in the Pakistani military and intelligence set-ups. Legend was that Daniel had stayed in Pakistan for 10 years under a Muslim identity, first as a student in Karachi University, then as a direct-recruit officer in the ISI (Inter-Service Intelligence, the Pakistani equivalent of the CIA) rising in the ranks for almost eight years till his cover was blown by an Indian intelligence agent who was caught by the Pakistanis in Nepal and tortured to death.

"Because after failing to get her own person as Chief Secretary," Daniel explained as if he was teaching alphabets to a 3-year-old, "she wanted to hit out at Government of India and paint India in a bad light. You just happened to present the perfect opportunity. Nothing personal against you, of course."

Alarmed, Raj looked at the PM who just smiled. Apparently, he too had been briefed about this wild theory.

"If that be true, Sir," Raj was not about to give up, "why did they let me go? Without attaining any of those objectives?"

"Oh, so you don't know?" Daniel asked. He then went on to explain the 'Operation Revenge' and how that left the Pakistanis with very little room for manoeuvre.

Raj was stunned. That the ever-so scrupulous Government of India could have an unconventional 'Operation Revenge' to be unleashed at a time of their choosing was too much to even comprehend.

At the same time, Raj was honoured that the Government of India had chosen to use this trump card for rescuing an insignificant IAS officer like him. But his reverie was cut short by a question, this time from the PM.

"So Rajji, what should be the next step now?"

"Sir," Raj replied, "I don't think I can work even one day with this CM. So, my request would be to let me go on leave till you give me a suitable assignment in Delhi."

"Rajji," the PM was still speaking softly, "I didn't ask for your personal preference, of whether you'd like to serve the J&K State Government or the Government of India. I want your advice on what India should do to J&K?"

"Sir," Raj thought for a moment, and then let it out in a torrent.

"I'd suggest we split J&K in three parts. Jammu and Kashmir as two separate States and Ladakh as Union Territory. That will hit Kashmiris like Hasina Ittoo really hard – Kashmiris who have properties in Jammu but who have chased away all Hindus from Kashmir. Kashmiris who want to spend their winters in Jammu but don't want Jammuwallas to spend their summers in Kashmir. Kashmiris who won't let cinema halls operate in Kashmir but have no qualms watching movies in Jammu."

"And Kashmiris who milk the GOVERNMENT OF INDIA for plan funds in the name of the more rugged and backward Jammu and Ladakh but who then divert all those funds to Kashmir," Daniel said.

"That's also true, Sir," Raj nodded.

"Supposing we agree to this spilt-idea, would you help us implement it then?" the PM said.

"Sir, with all the resources at my command," Raj replied, "but not with Hasinaji as CM. I won't then be allowed to move an inch."

"Who then?" Daniel asked.

"Actually Sir," Raj thought for a moment, "no Kashmiri will ever support this thought of splitting the State in three parts."

"So, is Governor's Rule the answer?" the PM asked.

"Under Mr Nohria?" Raj referred to the current 90-year-old Governor somewhat disparagingly. Mr Nohria had been a dyed-in-the-wool bureaucrat who could please all and annoy none. Consequently, political parties came and political parties went but he went on to occupy every important post under the Government of India – Home Secretary, Defence Secretary, Cabinet Secretary, and Principal Secretary to the PM. You name the post, and sure Mr Nohria would have held it at some point in his career.

"I get your point," the PM nodded.

Just then the doors opened, and a lady dressed in an elegant saree breezed in.

"Madam Monali Kumar?!" Raj gasped as he recognised his senior from the J&K cadre of the IAS and rose immediately to greet her.

"*Aaeye* Monaliji," the PM waved expansively. Do please come in. "And Rajji, meet your new Governor."

28

Delhi, Monday, 14 June 2021

AFTER exchanging pleasantries over a cup of coffee, the PM moved to his office and Monali and Raj followed him in another car. The cavalcade turned to the Janpath (People's Way) with the impressive National Museum on its right and the Jawaharlal Nehru Bhavan, the External Affairs office, on its left. It then turned left on the Rajpath (Kings Way) and zoomed through to the PMO in the South Block on the Raisina Hill.

At the PMO, Monali and Raj were ushered into a conference room where they met the Home Secretary Anil Saxena and the Principal Secretary to the PM Masood Hussain. Two stenographers joined in for taking dictations. The Constitutions of India and J&K were both kept on the table.

Raj as an old hand as Secretary to J&K Governor was tasked with the drafting of the report that the J&K Governor had to send to the Government of India requesting the imposition of the Governor's Rule in view of a severe 'breakdown of the law-and-order' machinery. There were some earlier drafts lying on the table. Raj just had to change dates and fill in some blanks, and *voilá*, a new order imposing Governor's Rule in J&K was ready.

Now came the trickier part. Home Secretary had to ring up Mr Nohria requesting him to put in his papers on 'health grounds'. And no one knew how the old man would react.

* * *

Mr Nohria was nursing his nightcap in Srinagar Raj Bhavan when his mobile rang. It was from Anil Saxena, the Union Home Secretary.

Nohria put Arnab Goswami, who he was watching on TV, on mute and picked up the call.

"Oh, hello Anil, how're you?"

"Good evening Sir. Sorry to bother you at such a late hour. But there was an urgent matter that couldn't wait."

"Okay...."

"Sir ... I don't know how to put it but this latest crisis – of abducting your Chief Secretary – has put tremendous pressure on us to take some decisive action ... action that is in line with the image of the Honourable PM to take tough decisions in an hour of crisis."

"All right ... and what do I need to do to help here?"

"Sir," the Union Home Secretary paused for a moment and then blurted out, "I don't know ... but the Honourable PM has decided it will look good if we let both the CM and the Governor resign."

Nohria gulped his brandy so hard that he choked. This was the call he was dreading all this while in his third term of Governorship in J&K.

"Are you okay Sir," asked the Home Secretary.

"Yes … yes, Anil. Tell me what exactly do you expect me to do?"

"Sir, on your secure line, we are sending two draft faxes. One, a proclamation from you – dismissing the J&K Government – for causing a breakdown of constitutional machinery on the law & order front. And secondly, your resignation as J&K Governor on account of ill-health."

"And Sir," the Home Secretary continued, "the Honourable PM has asked me to assure you that he holds you in his highest esteem and looks forward to using your experience in some other responsibility soon."

Nohria sighed. That was, he knew, bureaucratic mumbo-jumbo for him to behave. Or else.

"That's absolutely fine with me, Anil. I'm indeed a little tired of J&K after spending thirteen years here in the Raj Bhavan. So, resigning on grounds of ill-health, which is not entirely untrue, is actually a good idea."

"Sir, the faxes then are just being sent."

"Anil, hold on for a second," Nohria said as he remembered something. "Who are you sending in my place?"

"Sir, we are still working on that," replied the Union Home Secretary.

"In that case, may I request you to give me a week to pack up my personal stuff? I can pack up in Srinagar in two days and take another 4-5 days to pack my things up in Jammu. You know maintaining two Raj Bhavans in J&K means my personal stuff is scattered all over these two residences."

There was no response.

"Anil, are you there?"

"Sir, things are very fluid here. But I don't think we can spare more than three days for you in J&K. Please don't worry.

If anything is still left, I'm sure your successor will ensure that it reaches you safely and in no time."

"Anil, I've another problem. My personal bungalow in Gurgaon, which you know is given out to a diplomat. It will be a little difficult to throw him out before the rent agreement runs its course." Nohria now had opened another front.

The Home Secretary had anticipated this counter-move. The hint was that either you give me an official bungalow in Delhi or I go to town claiming how cruelly you treat a 90-year-old civil servant who had given his best years in the service of the Government of India.

"Sir, we'll ensure that the Governor's suite in the Jammu and Kashmir House on Prithviraj Road is made available to you as long as you need it."

"That will help somewhat," said a disappointed Nohria, knowing very well that the moment he quit as J&K's Governor, the staff in J&K House in Delhi too would stop treating him like the Governor. Which also meant that they will start charging him for his food bills and may even for his stay, which used to be free till now. This won't do. But beggars can't be choosers, can they be?

"Sir, the faxes have just been transmitted," the Home Secretary said.

"Yes, I can see them. Please hold." Nohria asked his attendant to pick up those two faxes which the machine in his first storey bedroom had just churned out. A few minutes later, the faxes were with him.

Nohria flicked through the draft. "They look fine, Anil. Don't worry. I'll take them from here."

"Thank you, Sir, and Good night." Relief in Home Secretary's tone.

"Good night Anil. And see you soon in Delhi."

Not with the request to get another gubernatorial assignment, sighed the Home Secretary as he disconnected the call.

*   *   *

Nohria buzzed his attendant to connect him to his Principal Secretary and asked the latter to fetch the Private Secretary and the Press Information Officer attached to the Raj Bhavan.

Within half an hour, the Governor's report recommending the imposition of Governor's Rule for a period of six months under Section 92 of the Constitution of Jammu and Kashmir, was sent to the President with a copy to the Prime Minister. Normally, for 'failure of constitutional machinery' in any other State of India, it is the President's Rule which is imposed under Article 356 of the Constitution of India. But in case of J&K, to appease the pro-autonomy lobbies, Nehru, India's first Prime Minister, had agreed that this Rule be called Governor's Rule, even though it had to be approved by the President of India! And in both cases, the President's Rule as well as the Governor's Rule, the files have to go through the Prime Minister and the Union Cabinet, because the President of India can act only on the advice of the Council of Ministers.

So, the file for concurring with the Governor's recommendations was first accepted by the Prime Minister, who sent it then to the President for his approval. The President, who was fast asleep, had to be woken up to accord his assent. The ninth Governor's Rule in J&K thus came to be imposed from Tuesday 15 June 2021.

Nohria was in two minds to inform Hasina Ittoo about this impending disaster. He had great personal relationship with the Ittoo family from the time he was Home Secretary under Mufti Saheb, Hasina's father. And he was not sure whether playing Government of India's game behind Hasina's back was going to get him anything in return at all.

In the end, Nohria decided in favour of calling up Hasina Ittoo who was fortunately awake watching a late-night TV serial.

"Governor Saheb," CM Ittoo sounded more irritated than surprised, "*sab khairiyat*?" All's well, I hope?

"*Nahin* Hasinaji." No, Madam Hasina. "Actually … this Chief Secretary's abduction hasn't gone down well in Delhi. And there are clamours for someone's head to roll."

"What!?" CM Ittoo was now fully alert. "Even when that idiot Chief Secretary has returned unharmed?"

"Hasinaji, the story is that the Chief Secretary escaped on his own, with nil help from our police…. But anyway, that all is immaterial. Because now the orders are that I impose Governor's Rule."

CM Ittoo who had put her TV on mute, now switched it off, and screamed,

"Governor Saheb, you do that and there will be hell to pay here. There will be *khoon ki nadiyan* (rivers of blood) in Kashmir's streets, literally, let me assure you. But you know that better than anyone else, don't you?"

"I know Hasinaji, but my hands are tied," Nohria said in an exhausted voice.

"Governor Saheb, this is not fair. You have had family relations with us for over 40 years, and it's time you let these Delhiwallas appreciate the *nazakat* (sensitivity) of the situation here. You know very well that we alone dare to carry India's flag. If you remove us, then … no force can stop Kashmiris from going to the other side (Pakistan)."

"Sorry Hasinaji. The arrow has left for its target, and I'm not the one releasing that arrow in the first place." Nohria tried to be philosophical.

There was silence for a moment as CM Ittoo was obviously mulling over her options.

"Hasinaji, are you there?" Nohria's voice was anxious.

"Yes, Governor Saheb ... one last thing then. How much time do I get to wind up my affairs?"

Nohria knew what that meant. It meant if she would be required to vacate her official residence *Fairview* at Srinagar's Gupkar Road, if she could quickly 'dispose off' some files where huge pay-offs were promised for her party's coffers, if she could cart away some nice furniture that she had only recently got for her office, to her ancestral home in Bijbehara....

"Sorry Hasinaji. The President of India's assent has just landed on my table, and, therefore, I've no option but to sign the proclamation right away."

As there was a hushed silence on the other side, Nohria bid CM Ittoo good bye and disconnected the call.

29

Srinagar/Delhi, Thursday, 17 June 2021

EXACTLY three days later, on June 17, 2021 at 0745 hrs, Nohria boarded the 8-seater Super King Air-350, the lone fixed-wing aircraft that the J&K Government possessed. There was no cabinet to see him off at Srinagar Airport as he had dismissed that cabinet only two days back. The J&K Home Secretary was there along with three other senior Secretaries, but the Chief Secretary hadn't turned up. Ostensibly he was sulking in Delhi after his so-called abduction.

Still, Nohria was grateful that he was not travelling alone – there were three officials of the Raj Bhavan in the plane, Vipul, his Principal Secretary, Rajendra, his butler, and Ashok, his PSO.

"Some coffee, Sir," the butler asked the moment the aircraft had attained cruising altitude.

"No, thank you Rajendra." The small aircraft had no toilet, and Nohria didn't want his bladder to act up after downing some coffee.

The King Air landed in the Technical Area of the Delhi Airport around 0900 hrs. Surprisingly, Raj Verma the Chief Secretary was waiting to receive Nohria there.

"Good morning, Sir," Raj greeted as Nohria alighted from the State aircraft, "I'm so sorry I was not there in Srinagar to arrange for a proper send-off."

"Oh ... that's okay. I learnt you were on leave."

"Yes Sir ... just gathering my wits after that traumatic episode," Raj said as he opened the left back door of the Governor's sedan that was waiting on the tarmac.

Nohria shook Raj's hands and got in the car. Raj saw the PSO getting in to occupy the front passenger seat of the Governor's car and the butler getting inside the back-up car but Vipul, the Principal Secretary kept standing on the tarmac. He, like Raj, was obviously waiting to accompany the new Governor back to Srinagar.

"Makes sense," Raj thought as he waved goodbye to Nohria's departing cavalcade.

* * *

At 0925 hrs, another cavalcade entered the Technical Area. Raj and the Principal Secretary to the Governor rushed but before they could reach the left rear door, a beaming Monali had herself opened the door and was out on the tarmac.

"Hello Raj, hello Vipul," she addressed both with a smile.

"Good morning, Mam and welcome to the State," both said in unison. Surprised that the new Governor spoke more like a friend than like a dyed-in-the-wool 'Governor'.

"Should we get in?" Monali asked as the pilot rushed in to greet her.

"Yes Mam. We are ready to take off. Whenever you are?"

"Oh, I believe we're ready," Monali said as she marched towards the aircraft's built-in ladder.

Vipul couldn't help but notice that the Governor was elegantly dressed in a blue-black silk saree and was sporting a matching blue bindi on her forehead. Before she retired from the cadre, however, Vipul had found her wearing salwar-kameezes more often, which was what most women wore in J&K. So, what was the signal a saree meant to give? That someone not ashamed of representing India was finally stepping in?

Vipul was also surprised to find that the new Governor hadn't aged. She looked in her forties even though Vipul knew she was in her sixties. Most Governors – in fact – all Governors appointed in India looked like they were on their deathbed. But not Monali Kumar. She looked so … 'Un-Governor' like.

* * *

The moment the two suitcases of the new Governor were loaded in, the little aircraft closed its door. It then taxied leisurely to the main runway and was soon airborne. As the seatbelt signs switched off, the new Governor turned to Raj and asked, "So Raj, what's the situation on the ground?"

"Madam," Raj said, "I'll be frank. The situation is volatile. Looks like Hasinaji has let loose all her goons, who have brought the city to its knees in two days flat."

"Ah, so do you think there will be some problem reaching even the Raj Bhavan?" Monali asked.

"Maybe, Mam, although we have imposed a strict curfew around the Airport Road that we will travel upon. My advice, however, would be to take the State helicopter straight to Nehru Helipad from the airport…."

Monali turned towards her Principal Secretary. "And what do you think, Vipul?"

"Mam," Vipul nodded, "the situation on the ground is explosive, as the Chief Secretary says. It is as if we are back in the 1990s … the time when we couldn't go to office in our official cars, couldn't stay in our government houses … couldn't go to the market … couldn't even get our daily bread and newspapers…."

"Mam, our Jammu staff is very jittery," Raj said. "They are being shifted to hotels in protected areas, but they are all clamouring for going home … just like the Kashmiri staff who are already staying in their homes."

"Hmmm …," Monali thought for a moment. "What's the way out then? We can't restore Hasina's government, can we?"

"Mam, I agree," Raj said. "That may be a little hasty and premature. She has to be punished for what she did. But Mam, poor Jammuwallas too are being squeezed in the process."

"Okay …" Monali said, "so … just to be the devil's advocate, what will happen if we let them go and operate from Jammu?"

There was pin-drop silence as both officers pondered over this apparently blasphemous suggestion. There have been curfews for months together in Srinagar, but you still had to keep the Secretariat 'functioning' with the help of Jammu employees. That's how it had been done for donkey's years.

"Madam," Raj said, "then work will totally stop in the Secretariat in Srinagar."

"Hasn't it stopped already?" Monali asked. "And why should we waste government money for keeping and feeding our employees in Srinagar hotels?"

"Madam," Raj was alarmed, "but then we will have to let the officers too, to go to Jammu to supervise the staff."

"And Mam," Vipul said, "what will happen if the Kashmiri staff too decides to go to Jammu?"

"Okay …" Monali said, "so what will happen if we shift the entire Secretariat to Jammu now? We improve productivity, solve people's problems, and save money, won't we?"

Both Raj and Vipul remained silent.

"Yes, it has never been done before.... Yes, this may give a signal that we have accepted defeat in Kashmir. But tell me, how do these perceptions matter when we have the larger good of our citizens in mind?"

The officers still looked flabbergasted.

"All right," Monali smiled. "Let's chew it over.... And Raj, I've decided that ... I won't travel by the State helicopter to reach Raj Bhavan. I'm returning to Srinagar after five years and I need to see if anything at all has changed on the ground.

"Second point, I don't want to deal with a *temporary* Chief Secretary. So please on landing, get my approval for making you a full-fledged Chief Secretary of J&K."

* * *

The morning was a little overcast as the State plane landed in Srinagar. As the new Governor stepped out, she was greeted with bouquets and ecstatic smiles from senior officers who had lined up, strictly in order of seniority, to greet her. There was palpable enthusiasm going beyond the standard protocol that the officers were supposed to observe. After all, they were witnessing history being created – of a cadre officer becoming the Governor in the same State that she had served for 37 years.

Raj walked along trying to introduce the officers, but that wasn't necessary as Monali was already addressing them by their first names. Reception over, the Governor was escorted to her official bulletproof car, and soon the huge cavalcade of some 30 vehicles, including those of the senior officers, was making its way to the Srinagar Raj Bhavan.

The journey was almost eventless, in an ominous sort of manner. All shops *en route* were closed. Some shopkeepers who lived nearby were sitting around hoping to get some signal that will permit them to open their shops. Every 500 metres, you could see a posse of helmeted policemen. Every crossing was littered with stones that jolted every vehicle that had to pass over them. Screams of 'Allah-u-Akbar' came from interior areas, as the wireless sets in the cavalcade crackled to indicate what was happening in which area.

Within 30 minutes, the cavalcade had reached Sonwar, the start of the 'safe zone', and the armed escorts heaved a sigh of relief. Journey thereafter on the Gupkar Road, past the Badami Bagh Army Cantonment gate, past *Fairview* the CM's residence, and past the Grand Hotel on the right, and golf courses on the left, up till the Srinagar Raj Bhavan, was now a breeze.

By 1115 hrs, as the BSF guards sounded the welcome bugle, the new Governor was alighting at the entrance of the picturesque Raj Bhavan where the Governor's staff had lined up to greet her. The view of the sprawling Dal Lake was breath-taking as ever, *especially when you couldn't see or smell the muck inside*.

A *shamiana* was erected over the lawns where the new Governor's oath-taking ceremony was to take place. At one end was a hastily put-out stage where two podiums were kept. One carried the emblem of Government of India and the other of the State of Jammu and Kashmir.

Seats for the guests were arranged in front of the stage. Most guests had already arrived and were seated.

Monali was ushered into the Governor's office as one ADC rushed down the steps to request the guests to settle down. At 1130 hrs sharp, both ADCs smartly turned out in their army uniforms escorted the new Governor to the dais where the Chief Justice of the High Court of J&K administered the Oath of Office.

That just took two minutes, where after J&K for the first time in its history had its first Lady and first J&K cadre IAS officer as Governor.

30

Srinagar, Thursday, 17 June 2021 (1)

THERE was a lavish High Tea after the Governor's 'swearing-in' ceremony, where the guests feasted on *seekh kebabs*, *bakarkhanis*, *samosas*, cakes, and sweet saffron-tinged Kashmiri *kehwa*. Senior officers from the Army, Air Force, State administration, police, and the intelligence agencies introduced themselves to the Governor. Interestingly, the political class was absent as they had all boycotted the ceremony. Even Hasina Ittoo, despite there being a reserved seat for her in the front row, had not turned up.

Half an hour later, as the ADCs signalled, the BSF band played India's national anthem, and everyone ceased talk and stood in attention. As they escorted Monali back to the Raj Bhavan, the guests started departing.

At 1230 hrs as planned, the Governor came to the conference room where the gathering included the top brass of J&K administration – the Chief Secretary, Director General of Police (DGP), Home Secretary, and the Finance Secretary.

"Gentlemen," as Monali waved the officers down to their seats, "I don't need you all to tell me that the situation is grave. But I'll be grateful if you could share any ideas. Of how we can restore, what we euphemistically call, 'normalcy' in the shortest possible time."

Monali cocked her head towards the DGP. "Suresh, tell me, how quickly can we round-up all miscreants?"

"Mam, in two days flat, if we are given the green signal," the DGP replied rather flamboyantly.

"Why two days? Take a week and stop all this nonsense. You now have the green signal, okay?"

Now the DGP looked worried. "Mam ...," he stammered, "does the green signal apply to the political bigwigs too ... you know the Hurriyat guys, members of the erstwhile cabinet, including their Chief Minister, the anti-national journalists...."

"Why do you look worried, Suresh?" Monali queried, "I thought the JK Police had an established drill to deal with all such things."

"Yes Mam," the DGP replied, "but the usual drill is that we keep the bigwigs under house arrest and the riff-raff in jails. Do you want us to do anything different or special this time?"

"That is for you to decide, Suresh. But I suppose you don't want to do the reverse – put the bigwigs in jail and the riff-raff under house arrest?"

The DGP blinked as the other officers suppressed a smile at the Governor's apparent sarcasm.

"What I mean to say, Suresh," Monali was back to her soothing self, "is that the JK Police has all the tools, the manpower, and the intelligence. So, you are the best judge. Don't expect *me* to micromanage your operations because as you will soon see there is an awful lot on my plate already."

As the DGP nodded his head in agreement, Monali turned towards the Chief Secretary.

"And Raj, tell me how you can make our Secretariat functional soon?"

"Mam," the Chief Secretary said, "actually I've been thinking hard about your Jammu idea … that just to teach the Kashmiris a lesson, we ask all Jammu employees to go to Jammu and make the Secretariat functional there. Then we will ask the Kashmiri employees to do the same after giving them a week to pack up their stuff. If they refuse, we will take action as warranted under rules for unauthorised absence, defying government orders, etc etc."

"And what will be the implications of this plan?" Monali asked. "Is this workable? Especially when we know that over 70% of Secretariat employees belong to the Kashmir Valley?"

"Yes, Mam," the Chief Secretary nodded his head, "the plan is too revolutionary or unconventional to even contemplate. It is alright to give a signal we mean business, but to make the Secretariat really functional in Jammu would mean that we pack all our records in Srinagar and move them to Jammu. Physically. Even for our well-planned bi-annual *durbar* moves, this exercise takes almost a month."

"Hmm …" Monali looked around. "Any other views?"

Everyone had fallen silent as the enormity of this unthinkable move hit them hard.

"Mam," it was the Home Secretary this time. "Won't this move give a signal to the international community that we have given up on Kashmir?"

"And Navin," Monali queried, "what do we gain by shutting everything down here for two months? What kind of signal will we be then giving to the international community?"

As the Home Secretary pondered over the query, the Finance Secretary piped in, "Mam, if I may?"

"Yes, Malay," Monali nodded.

"Mam, this early and wholesale move back to Jammu will have some financial implications ... which I must highlight. The disturbed conditions here mean that our tax collections will come down drastically, but moving employees to Jammu would mean increased expenditure on packing of files and their transportation, meeting the travelling allowance of employees, running air conditioners in Jammu as the monsoons are still some 15 days away.... So, in financial terms, this will be a double whammy ... that our precarious State resources can ill-afford."

"Okay Malay," Monali paused, "so how do we solve your problem?"

"Mam," the Finance Secretary replied, "since we are all here thinking of out-of-the-box solutions, we could first hit out at all employees who don't join their duties in Jammu. And stop their salaries till they do that. That will be a temporary relief – temporary because we will have to eventually pay them their dues after sanctioning leave of whatever kind due to all such absentees. A bigger relief could be if we dissolve the Legislative Assembly because then we will have huge savings on the salary, allowances, loans, and even medical treatment of our Honourable MLAs."

"That's a good suggestion," Monali said, "but this latter move will also hit out at our MLAs from Jammu and Ladakh regions. So, let me chew over it. Any other ideas?"

"Mam," the Finance Secretary had another thought coming. "We can also use this opportunity to recover all State dues on account of rent, taxes, bills, especially from all those influential businessmen, aligned to the ruling political dispensations, who have been avoiding them for ages."

"You can go full ahead on that front," Monali smiled, "and the DGP will give you all the assistance you need."

"Mam," the DGP said, "I'll be happy to do that. In fact, I could give the finance department CRPF for such operations that I could free by withdrawing them from their current duties of guarding the Hurriyat and other useless politicians. I may not save any money, but I'll earn a lot of goodwill among my CRPF colleagues who just hate guarding such anti-national elements."

The meeting was now warming up as more suggestions flowed in – and they ranged from being ludicrous to outrageous to everything in between. Suddenly, the DGP's mobile vibrated in silent mode. He looked at the message, and said, "Sorry Mam, but there is an urgent message from the IG of the RPF, the Railway Protection Force you know, to the effect that a violent mob has burnt down four bogies of the local train near Nowgam in Srinagar. They, the Railways, therefore, are scared to run any more operations and are requesting permission to relocate all their personnel and rolling stock beyond the tunnel in Banihal till the situation improves."

"Yes," Monali said without a moment's hesitation. "They have the permission to do that. And Suresh, please ensure that no such damage occurs to Railway personnel or property from now onwards."

"Yes, Mam," the DGP said as he rose to walk out of the room to call the IGP Railways to convey the instructions.

"Just a minute, Suresh," said the Governor, "I also want you to launch a special mission to catch that fellow … what's his name … yes, Abu Farzana, who had dared touch your Chief Secretary … dead or alive … Okay?"

"Yes Mam," acknowledged the DGP with surprising enthusiasm. Raj was deeply touched. *Here was a born leader that one could lay his life for.*

"And Raj, before I forget, when is the Amarnath Yatra concluding?"

"On 22 August Mam, when Rakhi falls. It's a Sunday, I believe. We are, therefore, all ready to start the 2-month yatra from 24 June, which is *Jyestha Purnima*."

"Okay, I'm sure the politicians will have no qualms unleashing their favourite terrorists to kill a few hapless pilgrims. So, Raj and Suresh, and Vipul as CEO of the Amarnath Shrine Board, please leave no stone unturned to ensure a trouble-free yatra."

"Yes Mam," all three said in unison.

It was almost 1330 hrs.

"Let's have lunch," Monali said as she buzzed her attendants to come in.

Within five minutes, piping hot vegetarian almond soup was being served to the gathering. Soup done, the entrée of baked trout arrived. The staff had to be commended to know what the new Governor liked. For the DGP, who was a strict vegetarian, the trout was expertly replaced by baked *paneer*.

As the gathering dug into the exotic entrée, an ADC walked in with an envelope. As the Governor gestured, the ADC opened the envelope and handed the card inside to the Governor.

It read:

> *Muhtarma Hasina Ittoo, and the members of the erstwhile cabinet of the Government of J&K, request the pleasure of Her Excellency the Governor of Jammu and Kashmir, Mrs Monali Kumar IAS (Retd), at dinner at 8PM tonight on Thursday June 17, 2021 at Fairview, Gupkar Road, Srinagar.*

A faint smile creased the lips of the Governor, as she pondered over this exercise of power play. This group had boycotted the morning swearing-in function of the new Governor, which was an *apolitical* event, but was now waving the white flag by inviting the same 'agent of the Government of India' for dinner.

It didn't take even one minute for the Governor to make up her mind.

"Please convey my regrets to Ms. Ittoo … and tell her that I'm rather busy with some important briefings today."

31

Srinagar, Thursday, 17 June 2021 (2)

"OKAY," Monali said as the main course of *Jeera pulao*, thick chicken curry, mixed vegetables, and apple *raita* was served.

"So, where were we? Yes, making the government functional in Jammu...." Monali turned towards the Chief Secretary. "Raj I think you should work on moving everyone to Jammu after seven days from today. And, this will not be a secret operation. Let everyone know about it, and comment on it as they deem appropriate."

"And Suresh," Monali now addressed the DGP. "Please withdraw all Government of India forces like ITBP, SSB, CRPF from politicians including the Hurriyat. And replace them with JK police. The anti-nationals don't really deserve this kind of protection. And I think no proponent of *azaadi* or self-rule can openly protest about this move. These Government of India forces instead should be deployed to guard all our vital installations and non-Kashmiri employees."

"And Malay," Monali turned towards the Finance Secretary, "you move on shoring up our finances. And let me chew over this idea of dismissing the Legislative Assembly to help save money. But meanwhile don't relent on recovering all loans, car loans, housing loans, computer loans ... given to legislators, dead or alive, with full interest and penalties as applicable.

"Also, see that we don't pay anyone, our employees, our suppliers, our contractors ... in cash. This would reduce our dependence on cash drastically as also the pressure on banks to maintain huge cash balances to service government operations which makes them an attractive target for terrorists."

"And Navin," Monali now addressed the Home Secretary, "you were supposed to head that committee to identify the corrupt and what you call ... the deadwood in government. Take out that report and finalise that fast so that we are able to save some money on that front too."

"And Raj," Monali turned towards the Chief Secretary, "while we are on this topic of saving money, please constitute a committee to identify all appointments, which have been made by our politicians illegally ... including the appointments in government-owned companies, societies, universities, hospitals, etc that bypassed all duly constituted recruitment agencies like the Public Service Commission (PSC) or the Sub-ordinate Services Recruitment Board (SSRB).

"There could be many more ideas for saving money as well as increasing our efficiency. So Raj, please organise a meeting...." Monali looked at the wall clock on the opposite wall and said, "say at 1530 hrs today in the Secretariat ... so that I can meet other officers and pick their brains."

"Yes Mam," the Chief Secretary said.

"And please ensure that no one, not even the Secretariat union guys, greet me with bouquets of flowers."

The caramel custard had just arrived. As Monali served herself a teeny-weeny slice, the Chief Secretary piped in, "Mam ... one last clarification. Would you be appointing some advisors to exercise the powers of the erstwhile cabinet?"

"No, Raj," Monali replied without hesitation. "I have no desire to bother with any advisors. And the avoidable expenditure on maintaining and humouring them. So, what we'll do is to empower all Principal Secretary rank officers to act as ministers. And you can carry out this exercise of allotting 4-5 departments to each such officer and get my orders today."

Lunch over, Monali got up.

"See you gentlemen then, at 1530 hrs today. I think I better get my unpacking organised."

As Monali climbed up the stairs to the first-floor residential area of the Governor, the ADCs escorted the senior officers to their vehicles, and saw them off.

* * *

At 1525 hrs, the Governor's motorcade had entered the premises of the 5-storey concrete building of the Srinagar Secretariat. Dull grey in colour – the building was nothing much to look at. Architecturally boring, but in its rectangular avatar it was ruthlessly functional. There were plenty of rooms for everyone. Officers of the rank of Additional Secretaries had independent rooms. While Secretaries and ministers had independent rooms with attached bathrooms and ante-rooms. The latter served the purpose of a lunch and siesta room as all such ante-rooms had a *dewan* to make lying down possible. Of course, this was also an excellent place to carry out all your shady deals, if you were so inclined.

As the obsequious security men opened the doors of the Governor's car, Monali got out and instinctively took to the stairs as she had done all her working life. The Chief Secretary, who was there to receive her on her maiden visit to the Secretariat, followed suit but everyone protested at the apparent 'breach of protocol' which was: how can the Governor climb the stairs rubbing shoulders with the hoi-polloi? So poor Governor was reluctantly herded back to a waiting lift, which took her to the third floor where the CM's office was located.

At 1531 hrs, the Governor entered the conference room. Nothing seemed to have changed. The painting behind the head of the table depicting – two hands holding the flag of J&K – was still there. Maybe the mikes on the table were new, but Monali wasn't even sure of that.

"Good afternoon, everyone," she said breezily as everyone greeted her back in unison. "Please do take your seats."

Monali sat in the CM's chair. "Okay, I'll come straight to the point. And that is – we have a crisis to manage. Just before coming here, I was picking up the brains of your Chief Secretary, DGP, the Home Secretary and the Finance Secretary and have received some feedback on how to make our Secretariat functional, how to cut down on our expenditure and how to shore up our resources. But I want thousands of such ideas. So, come on, shoot. Where do we start? May be with the power development department?"

Monali looked at the Power Secretary. "Yes Pramod, there you are. Tell me, what can we do about this perennial black-hole of a department that you head?"

"Mam," a startled Power Secretary said, "you know we have an age-old demand-generation mismatch." He paused gathering his thoughts. "In the sense that we generate hardly anything but have to buy power to meet our demand. Now adding more generation capacity is a long-drawn process, but certainly we can tackle our daily demand by enforcing *longer power cuts*."

The word power cuts took Monali back to her young officer days in Jammu. When her whole family had to suffer power cuts for as many as eighteen hours a day – in June when temperatures were above 45 degrees Celsius.

She remembered how her octogenarian old mother had turned an old newspaper into a handheld fan. But even that couldn't stop her from sweating. Monali remembered how her mother used to pray to the weather gods to bring in some rain. And repeatedly insisted that Monali called up the electricity department, which she had to, only to hear her calls going unanswered. Or worse, "Just give us half an hour" kind of reply when they'd been suffering for over seventeen hours.

Monali remembered her eight-year-old son asking her again and again, "When is the electricity going to come, mama?" And she had no answers.

"But aren't you in government? Aren't you supposed to know that answer?"

And she could only pat her son's hair to comfort him.

"Mama, why do we suffer such long power cuts? What's the reason?"

Oh yes, the reason? Demand-generation mismatch? The *stupidest* of stupid arguments. Monali came back to the present. No. This should no longer be the fate of the people of Jammu & Kashmir.

"Pramod!" Monali interrupted. "You're giving me the same reasoning that I've grown up hearing from the time I joined the J&K cadre, which was 40 years back. Why can't we do the same things that other better managed States do? For example, how has Himachal Pradesh, which is hillier than

Kashmir, become self-sufficient in power? How does Delhi manage its demand when it has to buy 90% of its needs from other sources?"

"Mam, that's because Himachal has a very enabling policy to encourage power generation in the private sector which we can't have in J&K for political reasons," the Power Secretary explained.

"That reason is gone, Pramod. So, can you do something now?"

"Yes, Mam, but...."

"No ifs and buts then. Just get me a draft ordinance tomorrow, for implementing the Himachal model here, I think that's the best model you have. I suppose you would have such a draft lying somewhere, won't you?"

"Yes, Mam...."

"And yes, as for demand management, I want you to implement the Delhi-Mumbai model, where every consumer pays by the meter. I know the politicians here have scared you to believe that if you did that, the Kashmiri public will lynch your meter readers. But tell me, if the Kashmiri can pay by the meter for his mobile, or his cable TV, and obscene amounts for educating his children in – fraud colleges in Bangladesh or Ukraine, why can't he pay for the electricity he consumes?"

"Mam, in the short run, arranging for so many meters would be a problem, both logistically as well as financially. I don't think the Finance Secretary would be able to accommodate me if I come up with a ₹ 100 crore demand for new meters tomorrow."

"Pramod, that's where I need you to get out of your politically correct approaches. And solve problems like an IAS officer. Where in the world does the power sector need government doles? You want meters? Then notify a few models, along with their authorised dealers in J&K, and ask consumers to get these installed at their cost directly, like any other electrical appliance that they buy. Upgrade your billing software so that – like the phone companies – your electricity is disconnected the moment your pending bills go past a certain level. Install prepaid meters like the ones that mobile, landline, or satellite direct-to-home TV companies have. There could be so many ideas. Is that clear?" Monali's voice was a little stern now.

"Yes, Mam," the Power Secretary nodded vigorously.

Monali turned to address all.

"Now for the other departments, who are not that much of a black hole as the power department has been, I'll lay down some basic principles. First, don't be a cry baby and solve your problems yourself with all the *jugaad* you have learnt so far as an IAS officer. Secondly, plug all leakages so that maximum benefit of our government efforts reaches our people. This, for example, means you can't have all your doctors, engineers, and teachers, regardless of how influential they are, posted only in the cities of Srinagar or Jammu."

Monali looked for reactions. Her audience seemed shell-shocked. No one had heard the Governor give such a strong message in a long time. In a very, very long time.

"Third, give me all the revenue you can earn, legitimately." Monali paused to take a deep breath. "For example, Traffic Police? Crack down ruthlessly on those who dare drive without licences, helmets, seat belts … whatever. But give me the amounts that you charge as penalty."

A few heads turned here and there as if the Governor had asked them to commit atrocities. Which made Monali suppress a smile.

"Any questions?"

One hand went up. It was the Secretary PHE or the Public Health Engineering Department.

"Yes, Sudhir," asked Monali.

"Mam ... ours is a department with nil revenue. What do you expect us to do then?"

"Sudhir, don't your rules provide for collecting water charges that all your compatriots in other States collect? So why can't you dust up those rules and get me those water charges that you have forgotten to collect till date? But please ... first graduate from a mere pipe laying department to a Public Health Engineering Department in all senses of the term ... that supplies really clean water to people."

"Public Works Department?" Monali now turned to the Secretary PWD. "Can you please try to get some of your important roads tolled so that we get some money to maintain those roads? And don't tell me that people here don't like to pay tolls, because to the best of my knowledge, they keep on paying some money to some authority on the road every few kilometres. Isn't it?"

Monali smiled as many others smiled and nodded in appreciation.

"Should I address some more departments?" asked Monali addressing no one in particular. As no one raised a hand, she continued,

"Okay ... Transport Department? Ensure that all your road worthy certificates and driving licences are issued in a transparent manner.

"Forest? If you can't give me money from the timber which in any case is looted away so brazenly then who can?"

"Fourth point." And she could see beads of sweat on some officers' foreheads.

"Reduce pressure on government machinery. So, Health Department, please join hands with our municipalities and focus on improving sanitation and hygiene so that diseases are stopped at the source.

"Education Department? See that our policies enable the opening of as many quality educational institutions as possible in the private sector.

"Industries? Forget central subsidies and tax holidays. Instead encourage ventures that don't spew smoke – like hospitals and educational institutions? Why can't our private sector hospitals and educational institutions be our new industries, and new destinations for tourists all the year around?"

There was some commotion as officers whispered to each other as to how the industrial lobby in J&K will react to such revolutionary ideas.

"Fifth point." Now some officers looked excited and enthusiastic. While others seemed like they were about to get a heart attack. "Focus on our strengths." Monali realised she sounded more corporate than bureaucratic. She cleared her throat to explain herself.

"Take up, for example, our handicrafts sector and see that nothing comes in the way to turning this into the most profitable sector for our craftspeople and the government.

"Tourism? Let's really become the Switzerland of South Asia, which you can't, unless you match the infrastructure and the fanatical obsession with cleanliness and punctuality that the Swiss have.

"Agriculture? Please think not just of rice, but of high value crops like flowers, European vegetables, mushrooms, Shah Jeera, saffron … let's supply to the entire world."

Monali stopped. She realised if she said more, some would definitely get a cardiac arrest.

"Friends, I think that should be enough for today. I understand you will have questions, which I suggest you should first take to your very able Chief Secretary. That will be all for today. Thank you."

With that, the Governor got up to leave for her office chamber which was next door. Raj and Vipul accompanied her with the proposals for merging departments and bestowing the powers of Cabinet Ministers on six Principal Secretary level officers, and of Ministers of State with Independent Charge on fourteen Commissioner Secretary rank officers.

"Raj," the Governor suddenly remembered something, "Wasn't it you who had some twenty years back carried out an exercise to merge departments in line with the set-up that prevails in the Government of India?"

"Yes Mam, but no one acted on that proposal."

"I know," nodded Monali, "because the politicians here like to harp on their perennial-shortage-of- officers theme. So, on one hand they like to *deport* officers to Delhi who don't toe their lines. And on the other, they want to recall all officers who are in Delhi because they think this will harass them and make them beg for mercy."

"That reminds me, Mam," Raj's face brightened up, "what do you want me to do about the letter the ex-CM had written to the PM asking to *return* all our officers? Because how else can she tackle militancy, she had added."

"Withdraw it forthwith," the Governor's response was sharp and instantaneous.

"Instead dust out that study of yours, because I remember you arguing that if one Secretary of the Human Resource Development Department in Delhi deals with higher, technical, and school education, we can't here have three Secretaries dealing with these same departments. Similarly, if one Secretary in Delhi deals with agriculture, horticulture, sheep husbandry, fisheries, and floriculture, we can't have five here."

"Yes Mam," replied Raj, "I remember suggesting that the general principle should be that because we don't have enough officers, a J&K Secretary here should be tasked to deal with 3-4 Secretaries at the Government of India level but not the other way around. Only this way can we have better co-ordination with the Central Government and benefit from all those great centrally sponsored schemes. This streamlining will also, I had hoped, free officers for field assignments which is where IAS officers, in my opinion, should be in the first 20 years of their career."

"I agree with you one hundred percent," nodded Monali, "and desire that we act on that exercise immediately."

Just then, there was a buzz on the intercom. It was the ADC. "Mam, the security at Raj Bhavan informs that Hasinaji, the ex-CM with two of her ex-cabinet colleagues, has just landed at the outer gates. They have been informed that you are not in, but they insist that they will then wait for you in the Raj Bhavan. What should we do?"

"Please escort them to the drawing room and serve them tea," the Governor couldn't help suppress a smile. "And yes, tell them that I'll try to meet them as soon as possible."

"And Raj, let's now quickly have a look at your proposals for reshuffling the administrative machinery."

With that, Monali returned to the permutations and combinations being worked out to ensure that officers of integrity manned all important posts. The exercise now was trickling down to the district level with the Governor insisting that all posts of Deputy Commissioners be manned by IAS officers as prescribed under the IAS (Cadre) Rules. Ditto about all posts of District Superintendents of Police that had to be filled from the IPS. And all posts of District Forest Officers by Indian Forest Service officers only. So, the Secretaries of the General Administration Department, Home, and forests had to be called in, along with the Director General of Police (DGP) and the Principal Chief Conservator of Forests (PCCF).

"Go by the rule book strictly and don't bother whose cronies get hurt in the process," desired the Governor.

It took almost an hour to finish this exercise. As she looked at the wall clock, it was almost 5 PM.

Time to now meet the ex-CM.

Monali called her ADC. "Saurav, please get the motorcade ready."

32

Srinagar, Thursday, 17 June 2021 (3)

AS Monali got down from her bullet proof black Ford Endeavour SUV, she was startled to see the ex-CM pacing up and down the sprawling verandah of the Srinagar Raj Bhavan.

"Ah Monaliji, there you are," Hasina Ittoo shouted, even before the Governor had time to catch her breath.

"Hasinaji, *sab khairiyat*?" Everything all right?

"*Kehan* Monaliji." Not really, Madam Monali. The ex-CM replied, as she walked alongside the Governor to the drawing room. "You know how this Mr Nohria, your stupid predecessor, has spoilt everything by dismissing my government and murdering democracy."

"But Hasinaji that is 3-day-old news. Why complain now?"

"Because we have such a sensitive lady like you at the helm of affairs now. Otherwise who would pay heed to the cries of poor, hapless Kashmiris like us?" said the ex-CM in chaste Urdu.

Sensitive lady? Monali remembered her own days in service in J&K when the very same politicians had accused her of being 'arrogant' and not understanding 'Kashmiriyat'. Or Kashmir's sensitivity.

As Monali entered the drawing room and reached her designated chair, the two ex-Cabinet Ministers got up and greeted her warmly.

"Monaliji, welcome to Kashmir. We have really missed you from the time you left us some five years back," gushed Muzammil Beg, the ex-Law Minister. His beard had grown whiter, his head balder and his eyes madder, as the Governor couldn't help noticing.

"Yes, Monaliji," added Mr Graboo, the ex-Finance Minister. His beard seemed to have become longer and girth wider. "The State very stupidly lost the services of such a bright and upright officer like you. Wish we could do something to retain you here."

"Anyway, that's so much water down the Jhelum under the Zero Bridge," Monali smiled, remembering how pleased these guys actually were to let her retire and leave the State. "But tell me, what kept you all away from today's swearing-in function in the morning? I certainly missed exchanging notes with you...."

Graboo looked at Beg, and Beg looked at Hasina, and all three looked decidedly uncomfortable.

"Please don't take it personally, Monaliji. You know how much regard and love we all have for you ... but that was all political," Beg blurted out, "I believe ... I must say, we were ill-advised."

You obviously were, you fools; otherwise you won't have swallowed your pride and come to me with your tails tucked between your legs, so soon!

"Doesn't matter," Monali said, "but let me offer you some tea ... at least I need a cup quite badly."

And as if on cue, small pea and potato filled *samosas*, sugar-sprinkled cupcakes, and salted assorted nuts were produced by the liveried bearers of Raj Bhavan.

As the tea was poured in fine china cups, black tea with lemon for the Governor, and tea with lots and lots of milk for the guests, Monali made small talk by sharing her first impressions of the city, how warm it had become that you needed to run air-conditioners in Raj Bhavan, how the Dal was still not clean, how the encroachments on the Airport Road appeared to have multiplied....

For the next three minutes or so, the guests munched on samosas and sipped tea, and complimented the Governor on her observations about the deteriorating civic conditions of the city.

"But what to do, Monaliji, *haalaat hi kuch aise the*," Beg said. The situation only was like that.

The ex-CM was, however, getting impatient.

"Monaliji," she interrupted, "we have come to protest about this blatant murder of democracy in the State. And to request you that you leave no stones unturned to restore it."

"But Monaliji," Graboo added, "instead we hear that you are thinking of moving the Secretariat itself to Jammu, which if true, will make the situation much more explosive."

"What's your suggestion then, Hasinaji?" Monali ignored Graboo and addressed the ex-CM. "The administration is totally paralysed. Jammu employees are fearing for their lives. If we don't take decisions now, whatever is left of the small working season in Kashmir, and Ladakh, will be totally lost. I don't think any of us would like to permit that."

"But what's new about that Monaliji? This is routine. Every year, during the summers, when the Secretariat is here, there are *hartals*, protests, stone pelting, shut downs ... how else do you expect people to voice their grievances ... to express their anger and frustrations?" Hasina replied.

"But tell me, Hasinaji, and this I've always wanted to ask," Monali countered. "What do Kashmiris really want? I've also watched the situation here for over 40 years and still don't know what people are angry about?"

"Come on, Monaliji," Beg interjected, "don't you know anything about the games Delhi has been playing with us?"

"For example, promising plebiscite to know whether the people wanted to go with India or Pakistan?" Monali asked.

"Yes, it all starts from there, and the UN resolutions too promised that," Beg nodded.

"But Beg Saheb, why did the plebiscite then couldn't be conducted? You are a lawyer, and you know well what the UN resolutions mandated ... that first, Pakistan had to vacate the whole of J&K ... which never happened. So why don't you explain this legal position to your people? And tell them to go pelt stones at the Pakistani High Commission instead?"

"Come on, Monaliji. It's not just history. People are also protesting about lack of jobs, shortage of electricity, broken water supply lines, absent doctors, and teachers ..." Beg said.

"Okay," Monali nodded, "then why are people in Jammu and Ladakh not protesting in a similar manner? Either about the *maslay-e-Kashmir* (the Kashmir problem) or the civic problems that you mention?"

"Because they don't have so much army breathing down their necks," Hasina piped in, "look how many thousand have been blinded by their indiscriminate use of pellet guns."

"But Hasinaji, the army doesn't use pellet guns. And the forces that use these guns, are either your own JK Police or the CRPF, under your command ... and I suppose they use those guns mostly in self-defence, in situations when the mobs are out to lynch them. But I'm sure each such case of pellet blinding would have been investigated by your government. Why don't you make those findings public?"

"But Monaliji," Graboo said, "there have been so many cases where enquiries have established that army men have killed innocents for getting rewards or medals. *Wo bhi koi doodh ke dhule thore hi hain.*" They too are not entirely blameless, colloquially 'washed in milk'.

"But Graboo Saheb," Monali argued back, "in every such incidence that you know of, the indicted have been punished, cashiered, demoted in rank, jailed, or even awarded capital punishment. But again, you only advertise the former fact of army men committing atrocities, but not of them getting indicted and punished so severely."

"So, Monaliji," Graboo was not willing to concede any ground, "do you think that justifies the use of AFSPA or the Armed Forces Special Powers Act?"

"Graboo Saheb," explained the Governor, "AFSPA to the best of my knowledge means that if the army is ever called out to conduct any operations, and any excesses allegedly happen in the process, they can be prosecuted only with the permission of the Government of India. This is just to ensure that they are not unnecessarily and often frivolously dragged into police stations and courts. But the main point is, if you don't like the army and the special protection that they have under AFSPA, don't declare any area as 'disturbed' and don't invite the army to conduct any operations. Simple?"

"Monaliji," Hasina was now getting irritated, "are you suggesting that Kashmiris are mad ... that's why they agitate without any reason? That they have not been discriminated? What do you think your Indus Water Treaty has done to our water rights?"

"Ah, the Indus Water Treaty," Monali almost sang. "Again, a question I have pondered over all my service in J&K. So, tell me Hasinaji, if you had joined Pakistan in 1947, what would have then happened to your riparian rights? Could Pakistan permit you to dam any Kashmiri rivers?"

"Why should we bother about such hypothetical questions," Beg interjected, "we are with India willy-nilly. So, we can take our grievances only to this big brother."

"Okay then, about the Indus Water Treaty, Beg Saheb," Monali asked, "I've always wondered that if it were scrapped tomorrow, where in Kashmir would you like to build your first dam? And drown so many villages?"

Beg was flabbergasted for a moment as submerging any Kashmir village was unthinkable.

"But why Kashmir? We are talking of the entire J&K. There are so many places in Jammu and Ladakh regions where we could dam a river but can't because of this blasted treaty."

"So why are people in Jammu or Ladakh not agitating about scrapping this treaty?" Monali countered.

"Because they are not as politically aware as we Kashmiris are," Graboo explained. "Jammuwallas are traders and would be happy if they could trade even with the devil. As for Ladakhis, they can't think beyond their daily dose of *chhang* (rice beer)."

The flippant generalised descriptions of the two other regions caught Monali off-guard, but she recovered and tried again.

"Coming back to the so-called Kashmir problem, tell me the real reason. The reason your young *fidayeen* (suicide bombers) keep on sprouting on social media…."

Every one fell silent.

"Let me articulate it then," Monali said, "what they say … basically … is that a Muslim Kashmir can't live with a Hindu, and thereby *kafir* (infidel) India, and that they shall not rest till they have the Islamic Rule here and their own Caliphate in accordance with the Shariat. Am I right?"

"Monaliji," Beg protested again, "you can't go by the rantings of a few radicalised and brainwashed youth. If we believed in that theory, we would have all wound up our political shops, and Hasinaji would have become *pardanashin* ... you know go behind a veil, and we would have all gone home to grow beards. So ... don't believe all that rubbish that circulates on social media."

"Monaliji," Hasina said impatiently changing the topic, "we have really been going in circles, away from the point we started with. Which is to seek your help to restore democracy here. As our own cadre-officer, tell us frankly if you can do that."

"Hasinaji," Monali replied, "I have NOT imposed this Governor's Rule, and I'm no one to order its revocation. But certainly, things can change if the premises underpinning the initial event change."

"Huh? ... And what were those?" Hasina blinked.

"The collapse of the law-and-order machinery that my worthy predecessor has quoted in his report.... Your Chief Secretary was abducted in broad daylight ... from a super secure Government Guest House ... minutes before a scheduled cabinet meeting under your *chairmanship* was to be held. And you think that was a joke? And what happened thereafter? It was complete mayhem on the streets. Markets remain closed. There was no transport. People still can't buy vegetables or baby food –"

"Monaliji," Beg interrupted, "this situation can only improve if we're back in the saddle...."

"And do you guarantee that?"

As Beg fumbled for a reply, there was silence all around.

"That settles it then. Now if you'll excuse me ... I had a rather long day today," Monali said as she got up and moved towards the Governor's office.

As the Governor sat down in her chair, there was a buzz on her intercom.

"Mam," her Private Secretary said, "there was a message from the Prime Minister's office. The PM would like to talk to you as soon as possible. Should I connect Mam?"

"Yes, please do," Monali nodded.

Just then there was a commotion at the main door as if the office attendants were trying to stop someone.

They obviously had failed as the doors flung open, and the ex-CM with tears streaming down her cheeks strode in.

Startled Monali got up and tried to make Hasina sit on the sofa. She poured her some water which Hasina sipped gratefully.

"Hasinaji," Monali implored, "please get a hold of yourself. It doesn't look good to lose control in front of so many of our junior staff."

Hasina kept sobbing. And kept accepting the tissues the Governor was offering to dab out her tears.

"Monaliji, I'm really heart broken. Of all people, I had expected you as a lady would understand the plight of another lady better. But you too are behaving so bureaucratically ... (sob) ... probably Hindus just can't appreciate the travails of what a Muslim woman has to go through when she is quoted verses from the Holy Book declaring that women were, by design, made deficient by Allah ... (sniffle) ... that she should never dream of ascending the throne ... and when women like Benazir Bhutto or Khaleda Zia take over countries like Pakistan or Bangladesh, everyone conspires to either kill them or remove them from power by hook or by crook.... Same is happening in

Kashmir. You can't imagine how lonely and miserable I feel … (sob) … you don't know how happy and gleeful my own cabinet colleagues are to see my discomfiture…."

"Hasinaji," Monali consoled, "please do control yourself, because you of all people know that I have not come to J&K to keep any seat warm. If I were interested in that, I'd have gladly accepted any of those Water Regulatory Authority or Electricity Commission posts that your government was very kindly considering me for. So, let me promise you … that I will leave no stone unturned to restore popular rule here, with hopefully you back in the saddle. But to help me plead your case in Delhi, please go all out to control those lumpen elements who are roaming our streets, provoking the forces. Please ask your party men, and everyone you know of, to stop paying thousand rupees or whatever is the rate today for pelting stones. Otherwise, we'll remain caught up in this cycle of violence that will never end, regardless of how many enquiry commissions you set up to find the real culprits. So, let's have a deal there – you bring peace to Kashmir, and I'll see that you get back your office room in the Secretariat immediately thereafter. What do you say?"

"Is that a promise, Monaliji?" Hasina asked stifling a sniffle.

"Yes, that is," Monali answered, and breaking protocol saw off Hasina Ittoo to her car.

33

Srinagar, Thursday, 17 June 2021 (4)

"MONALIJI?" It was the Prime Minister on the other side.

"*Namaskar* Sir," Monali answered, "sorry I couldn't call you earlier."

"Oh, that's okay. I just wanted to congratulate you on surviving your first day in the hot seat and…."

"That's very kind of you, Sir, but this is my old cadre, and I have seen worse times from some very unsecure positions."

"Monaliji," the Prime Minister was suddenly serious, "I understand Hasina Ittoo had come to see you with two of her cabinet colleagues. She would have, I'm sure, made quite a drama about the murder of democracy, and butchering of *Kashmiriyat*, and … but please don't get taken in by her tears."

Monali was stunned. She had seen off Hasina Ittoo just a few minutes back. And the report of her tears had already reached the PM! Did that mean that the IB had direct links in the *Raj Bhavan*? That there were moles among her own dumb-looking office attendants?

"No Sir, certainly not," Monali regained her composure, "I have a job to do, and I'm focusing on that."

"Good," the PM was back to his soothing self, "there is a report that the *Jammu Mukti Morcha* held a meeting today protesting against the harassment of Jammu employees in Srinagar ... and decided to intensify their struggle for a separate Jammu State. Would it be possible for you to go to Jammu tomorrow and talk to them?"

"Certainly, Sir," Monali answered without a moment's hesitation. "In fact, I was thinking of going to Jammu soon, but now that you speak of this emergency, I'll go there tomorrow ... in fact, I will go via Vaishno Devi as I'm technically the shrine board's new chairperson."

"That will be great. Jammuwallas will, I'm sure, appreciate this gesture of invoking the blessings of Goddess Vaishno Devi very much.... Anything else you would like us to do?" asked the Prime Minister.

"Sir, as we had discussed, we need to make the Jammu Secretariat functional ASAP. Tomorrow, in Jammu, therefore, I'll like to meet some solar energy experts who can install solar panels on the rooftop of all buildings in the Secretariat complex along with some energy-efficient hot-and-cold inverter air conditioners so that the Secretariat there becomes immune to the vagaries of weather."

"That is a great idea, Monaliji. I'll just ask my Ministry of Renewable Energy Secretary to organise it. I don't know why J&K was using its Article 370 to keep away from India's solar revolution too. Is that all?"

"For the time being, yes Sir."

"Then bye for now, Monaliji, and wish you once again the best of luck." And with that there was a click on the secure line.

34

Vaishno Devi, Friday, 18 June 2021

AT 0800 hrs, Monali was getting into her car to go to the Nehru Helipad when a commotion at the gate caught her eye. She cocked her head towards the Superintendent of Police, Raj Bhavan.

"What is it?"

"Mam, these are some Kashmiris wishing to see you. Some claim they've worked with you when you were in J&K. But for security reasons, I haven't let them in."

"What? Why have you stopped them," Monali exploded, "carry out whatever checks you need to, but let them meet me. That's the least I can do for my old staff."

The Superintendent gave a sheepish "Yes, Mam," and scurried away to carry out the orders.

*   *   *

Monali was surprised to see so many familiar faces. She recognised Ghulam Hassan immediately who was her ex-driver.

Fortunately, he hadn't become much balder than before. A blade of hair still remained on the back of his head. But his skin had wrinkled.

"How're you Ghulam Hassan?" Monali greeted him as he held her hand to kiss it.

Next, she met Shareef-ud-din, her office peon. Unlike Ghulam Hassan, he'd aged considerably. He wore glasses and his stubble had turned white. "Oh my God, Shareef-ud-din, is that really you?"

Shareef-ud-din nodded. Monali remembered him having a drinking problem. "Hope you're off-booze now." And Shareef-ud-din nodded again.

Monali then met Ashraf. He had worked as a clerk on her staff. She calculated he would be around seventy-years-old now but looked as energetic as he was in service. A young man stood next to him who looked exactly like Ashraf. That same sharp nose.

"And Ashraf, who is this young man you have brought along? Your son?"

"Yes, Mam, this is Mehraj," a beaming Ashraf replied, "and he just lost a bet because he was sure you won't recognise me."

"Ah, I know," nodded the Governor, "the great Kashmiri theory about the ungrateful Indian … but of course, I recognise all of you. How can I forget people who served me so loyally once?"

The rendezvous almost brought tears to Monali's eyes. She was touched that people who had worked with her such a long time ago – had braved so many odds to come to a 'marked' place like the Raj Bhavan, to meet her.

"Mam, the pilot is advising immediate take-off because of worsening weather over the Banihal Pass," the ADC whispered. That made a reluctant Monali get inside her car bidding goodbye to everyone.

* * *

By 0815 hrs, she had reached the Nehru Helipad. The two pilots ran to the Governor's car and opened the rear door.

"Sorry, gentlemen," Monali smiled, "are we ready to take-off?"

"Yes, Mam," the two ex-air force pilots shouted in unison as they rushed to start the twin engine Agusta-109E.

* * *

Within minutes, the big bird was airborne, cruising over the picture-postcard perfect Royal Springs Golf Course. It then turned towards the Grand Hotel, the oldest five-star hotel in Srinagar, gained height to cross the Zabarwan hills, and then headed straight towards the Banihal Pass.

Monali looked around and sighed to notice the brown Jhelum meandering as it had been for centuries. It was difficult to imagine that this lazy, languorous river had only a month back risen in anger to wreak havoc on Srinagar.

Green paddy saplings were everywhere. Looked like the resilient Kashmiris had recovered well from the floods. They may even have a bumper harvest, thanks to the new fertile soil dumped in by the flood waters.

Clouds over the Banihal rocked the flying machine, but the moment they crossed the treacherous mountain pass and were over Banihal town, things quietened down again.

By 0845 hrs, the State chopper had made it to Sanjhi Chhat, the helipad for the Vaishno Devi Shrine. It didn't switch-off its rotors, as usual, and after dropping Monali with her staff, flew down to Katra Helipad to park and await further instructions.

* * *

A huge crowd of Vaishno Devi Shrine Board's staff led by its CEO awaited to receive the Governor. After all, this was the first visit of their new chairperson, which the J&K Governor is ex-officio, to the shrine area.

A few ponies waited below the helipad to take the Governor in relatively greater comfort to the shrine, but she chose to walk. *En route*, she enquired about the welfare of many old employees and was sorry to learn that Trilochan, the Sub-Divisional Magistrate or the SDM, who used to escort her for *darshans*, had passed away. Pandit Shastriji, the Head *Pujari* (priest) had retired. The yatra was regularly crossing the ten million mark, thanks to the two new ropeways that were functioning well.

The place looked familiar but it saddened Monali to know that her old acquaintances were no longer around. Time changes everything.

* * *

In about half-an-hour, the Governor had reached the Governor's suite on the first floor of the Bhavan area. This was an elegant wood-panelled one bed room suite with a huge drawing-dining room attached to it. The big circular dining table often acted as the conference table for the times the Governor wished to meet senior functionaries of the shrine board there.

Governor had just a sip of fresh pomegranate juice when the priests or *pujaris*, led by the Head *Pujari*, arrived to escort the Governor for darshans of Mata Vaishno Devi. Chanting holy mantras, the priests marched ahead with the Governor and her entourage following behind. They had already shed their leather shoes, and worn rubber slippers, as leather is prohibited to be carried inside any Hindu shrine.

Just outside the shrine entrance, close to the golden statue of a magnificent lion, which the goddess rides to slay demons, everyone shed their rubber sandals too. On the right side, there still was the glass-panelled counting room where the cash offerings of the devotees were being counted in a very transparent manner, literally. The counting staff in their special white dress, that had no pockets by design, stood up to greet the new chairperson, which Monali acknowledged with a wave back and a smile.

Everyone then rung the metal bell hanging from the roof of the tunnel, announcing their presence to the deity, in an ancient Hindu ritual that the modern call bells seem to be inspired by. They then walked bare feet on the cold and wet marble floors leading to the Holy *Pindies* or the embodiment of the three goddesses.

Hope the Goddess grants me success in the special task I'm engaged in.

Although this must be her umpteenth visit to the Holy Shrine, the first sight of the three pindies representing Goddess *Kali* (the slayer of demons), Goddess *Lakshmi/ Vaishnavi* (the goddess of prosperity), and Goddess *Saraswati* (the goddess of knowledge) took Monali's breath away. Dressed in resplendent orange silk dresses, the goddesses indeed looked gorgeous. Everyone bowed their heads in reverence as the two priests sitting around the deity asked the Governor to sit down on the marble platform. They performed a special puja where after the blessed dignitaries made their way out through the exit tunnel back to the Governor's suite in Kalika Bhavan.

* * *

The CEO of the Shrine Board had organised a brief PowerPoint presentation on the latest developments that the Governor patiently went through. She had some questions on staff salaries and perks and her general instruction was that while they should be paid better than their counterparts in the

State Government, they have to be more disciplined and devoted than government employees.

Just then the Head Pujari arrived with the *prasadam* in the special wicker basket meant for VVIPs. The Governor's basket contained a traditional red *chunri*, that was once adorned by the goddesses, a blue-turquoise silk saree offered to the deity, a coconut, and a packet of assorted dry fruits like cashews, raisins, and almonds. There were *prasad* packets for everyone in the conference room, including the shrine board's CEO, which they all accepted with reverence.

Suddenly, the wireless sets crackling outside the Governor's suite went berserk. A security staff rushed in to whisper something in SP Raj Bhavan's ears. As Monali looked towards at him quizzically, he said, "Mam, information is that hundreds of agitators are marching towards the Jammu Raj Bhavan to present a memorandum to your good self. They have been held around *Kachhi Chhawani* area, about 200 metres from the Raj Bhavan, but they are growing restless. The police there want to know if they should use force to disburse the crowd."

"No!" Monali's response was unequivocal. "Just convey a message to their leaders that they should choose a group of five people to represent them. Duly escort them to the Raj Bhavan waiting room and serve tea. I think, I can make it to Jammu in another hour?"

"Yes Mam." The SP rushed out to alert the pilots.

"Has the Chief Secretary reached Jammu?" the Governor asked the ADC.

"Yes, Mam, and as you desired, he along with the Divisional Commissioner Jammu should be reaching the Raj Bhavan any moment."

"Good, let's leave then," said the Governor as she got up.

"Alok," she addressed the CEO, "I'll love to have a detailed pow-wow with you some time soon. I'll also like to ride the new ropeways and inspect the other important projects of the Board. But today, I have to rush. Okay?"

"No problems Mam," answered the CEO, "please just indicate your convenience and it will be our privilege to brief you."

"One thing more, Alok. As things are developing rapidly elsewhere, I want you to review the shrine's security threadbare. Please involve the army too. Can you do that tomorrow and let me know if you need anything more from the State Government's side?"

"Certainly Mam," replied the CEO, taking the hint immediately.

* * *

Monali's helicopter took off, swooping down in minutes to the over-built Katra Town first and then over the National Highway to Jammu Raj Bhavan. It flew over the picturesque Hari Niwas Hotel and the Amar Mahal Museum overlooking the Tawi River and landed plonk in the middle of the vast lawns of the Raj Bhavan.

35

Jammu, Friday, 18 June 2021

AS the rotors stopped, the pilots came out to open the passenger doors and Monali stepped out.

There was quite a crowd of Raj Bhavan staff – gardeners, sweepers, cooks, bearers, and security staff – to receive the Governor on her maiden visit to Jammu. The Head *Mali* (gardener) was carrying a beautiful bouquet in his hand which he rushed to present the Governor:

"Madam, *khushamdeed, yeh sab apne bag se hain"* (Welcome, these are all from this garden), he gushed.

"But then, Khan Saheb," Monali addressed the bearded gardener with respect, "why did you have to murder them?"

The elderly gardener didn't know where to look as the Governor handed over the bouquet to the ADC and marched to the foyer of the stately Dogra-era Raj Bhavan.

The Chief Secretary and the Divisional Commissioner, who also by then had joined the gathering, escorted the

Governor to her office room. As everyone took their seats, she addressed the Divisional Commissioner. "So Suraj, how's the situation here?"

"Quite under control, Madam," Suraj replied, "Jammuwallas are agitated but the only violence they've committed so far was to upturn a few police barriers."

"And how did the police react?"

"Mam, the police are on the edge, especially when all this was happening in front of the Police HQ in *Kacchi Chhawani*. That's why we have left the IG (P) Jammu there to control his men."

"That's good," Monali nodded in appreciation. "Now tell me who are these guys I have to meet now?"

The Divisional Commissioner was ready with the full dossier which he handed over to the Governor. As she leafed through, she was surprised that it was no longer a motley group of agitators acting as the Jammu *Mukti* (Liberation) *Morcha* (Front). This time, the Front had representatives from all political parties and was being led by Mr SK Sundal, who being an ex-Chief Secretary of the State had a reputation of being somewhat apolitical.

"Okay, this is not too bad," Monali nodded "should we meet them then?"

"Sure Mam," the officers said in unison as they stood up to escort her past the formal drawing room to the dining-cum-conference room where the delegation was seated.

* * *

As Monali entered, every one stood up to greet her folding their hands.

"Nice to see you Sir," Monali greeted Mr Sundal. Surprised that Sundal hadn't changed much. "As I see a lot of new faces today, may we start with a little round of introduction?" she asked.

That took some time, as each delegate gave his name, vocation, political affiliation, and the district he was representing. Mr Sundal filled in some more information, which if nothing else, indicated that his leadership position appeared to be unassailable.

"Monaliji," Mr Sundal addressed the Governor, "it is so wonderful to see a familiar face in the Raj Bhavan, especially one which has been famous for its fair and unbiased conduct.

"As you can appreciate, *Jammu Mukti Morcha* is no longer a motley group of people who used to create mayhem in the streets when you were in service. Instead it is today composed of representatives of all districts, all political parties, all faiths, all industry, and trade bodies ... you name it. And we are all united in our resolve to seek freedom from the communal, corrupt, anti-national, exploitative, and oppressive rule of the Kashmiris."

"Oppressive rule of the Kashmiris? Could you please elaborate on that?" Monali knew the answer having served 40 years in the State but she wanted to hear this straight from Mr Sundal's mouth.

Mr Sundal paused and took his time to word his reply. It was amazing – Kashmiris spent not even a second thinking about how they sounded. Maybe because they just had to play the victim card, claiming that it was always someone else's fault – India's, Pakistan's, or even Jammu's. *And poor hapless Kashmiris sandwiched in between had nothing to do with any of those problems.* But ask the same question to a Jammuwalla and he'll wipe his forehead with a handkerchief and think thrice.

"Monaliji, as we all know, we've always been hard core nationalists. Be it a Hindu or a Muslim ... in Jammu we've always waved the tricolour and not even once shouted pro-Pakistani slogans, since 1947. That makes us very different from Kashmiris. We hate it when our problems are referred to as the Kashmir problem. We hate it when the rest of India asks us why we want to join Pakistan. We hate it when funds that come for us get diverted to Kashmir because the problem is there."

Monali listened quietly.

"In Jammu, we are also communally much more integrated. Both Hindus and Muslims live together in all districts and unlike the Kashmiris who have chased away almost 99% of their Hindu brethren, we in Jammu have, since 1947-48, not thrown out even a single Muslim family ... despite the action of so many *agent provocateurs* sent by the communal Pakistanis and Kashmiris.

"Monaliji, you know, how those chased away Kashmiri Hindus still live in camps in Jammu in pathetic conditions. In fact, we assert that Kashmiri politicians have only paid them lip service and secretly ensured that they never come back. And now most can't go back because their houses and orchards have been taken over by our Kashmir-centric government and even demolished in the name of building better infrastructure.

"In Jammu, Kashmiris don't like that we Hindus and Muslims live harmoniously. They want to create a divide. Kashmiri politicians want the Muslim regions of Jammu to side with them. We're sick and tired of such communal politics."

Monali was about to say something but Sundal continued.

"There is no balance in our relationship," Sundal repeated himself for the second time. "Kashmiri Muslims want to spend their winters in Jammu. And nowadays many never return to Kashmir even during the summer months because their children attend coaching classes here. Look at Bhatindi. It looks like mini-Anantnag. The Kashmiri ghettoisation has ruined that place.

"But there is no reciprocity. Forget about working there. Jammuwallas cannot even dream of living in Kashmir during the summers, the way they used to some 30-40 years back. And on top of that, they're settling Bangladeshi and Rohingya Muslims in Jammu who are hardcore radical Islamists. No Islamic country wants to accept them but that is not stopping them from encircling Jammu. The Kashmiri leadership secretly wants to do the same thing to us which they did to their Kashmiri Hindu brethren some 30 years back. Sorry for sounding so communal."

"It's okay," Monali said. "You needn't apologise. But Sir, you know a State cannot be carved on the basis of religion."

"But what about on linguistic basis, Monaliji? States in India were constituted initially on linguistic grounds. So Marathis constituted Maharashtra, Tamilians Tamil Nadu, Punjabis Punjab, Malayalis Kerala.... On that same linguistic criterion, J&K deserved to be split in three parts: Kashmir for Kashmiri speaking, Jammu for Dogri speaking; and Ladakh for Ladakhi speaking people. But unfortunately, that never happened here."

Monali nodded.

"Some States were split for better governance. So, Bihar was split into Bihar and Jharkhand, Uttar Pradesh into Uttar Pradesh and Uttarakhand, Andhra Pradesh into Telangana and Andhra Pradesh.... Again, if we apply the governance criterion, then too each of our three regions need to be autonomous, as geographically they are huge, much bigger than many States. Ladakh, for example, is bigger than Kerala. Our geography is different and so are our developmental needs. You just cannot apply the low altitude sub-tropical Jammu development models to a high altitude cold arid desert like Ladakh."

"I can't dispute that," nodded the Governor.

"Thirdly," Sundal emphasised the word, "Jammu has always been under-represented. Jammu has more population than Kashmir but far fewer seats in the Legislative Assembly. Plus, our Chief Ministers have always been Kashmiris. Meaning our grievances are rarely addressed."

"Sundal Saheb, if I may ask," Monali interrupted, "all these grounds have existed for quite some time. What has then happened now that you have been forced to take to the streets?"

"Because," Sundal was ready with his answer, "never have Jammu employees felt so vulnerable in Srinagar. Tell me Monaliji, you have lived through those really difficult days in early 1990s when I as Chief Secretary couldn't stay in my own designated government bungalow in Srinagar. But did you ever hear of an attempt to kidnap or kill any non-Kashmiri employee? But this time with this attempt on the State Chief Secretary, we have lost whatever little confidence we had in our Kashmiri leadership. Don't you agree, Raj?"

As everyone looked to the Chief Secretary, he cast his eyes down and remained quiet.

"You do have a point there, Sir," Monali intervened immediately to reduce Raj Verma's discomfiture. "But tell me. Have you thought through your Statehood plans? This may be a new *Jammu Mukti Morcha*. As you say. Maybe some kind of improved version 50.0. But as I remember, all such earlier plans to separate used to fizzle out. Because of the great symbiotic relationship Jammu businesses had with their Kashmiri counterparts. Are you really willing to write those off – those age-old lending-borrowing, wholesaler-retailer, *wazwan*-relishing businesses? That you have shared so far with the Valley?"

"Madam," the President of the Jammu Chambers of Commerce spoke this time. "Unfortunately, those relationships are almost dead now. Kashmiris are constantly reneging on all business deals … on the ground that they have problems collecting their dues from customers who have taken our goods. Crores are thus stuck in the name of militancy. So, whether we separate from them or not, we have decided to have no further sale-on-credit relationship with the Kashmiris."

As many other business leaders nodded in agreement, Monali turned to Mr Sundal. "Separate Statehood is still a serious business, Sir. Have you thought through all the implications? For example, how will you manage your revenues and expenditures?"

"Yes Monaliji," Sundal replied, "unlike the Kashmiris, who think they are entitled to impose some kind of *jizya* tax on India, we have all been debating about our financial viability very seriously. Our model in this regard is our neighbour Himachal Pradesh. So like Himachal, we would first privatise all our hydro resources. That will get us revenues as well as make us self-sufficient in electricity production. And unlike the Kashmiris, we'll not harass NHPC but let them continue as our valued partners."

"Good point," Monali said.

"Next, we'll harness our huge pilgrim tourism potential. Vaishno Devi already gets more than a crore or 10 million pilgrims every year. We will now focus on getting those people to visit other religious places … like Shiv Khori, Sudh Mahadev, Sukhrala Devi, or Buddha Amarnath. Or tourist places like Patnitop, Kud, Sanasar, Mansar, Surinsar, Bhaderwah, and so many picturesque places in the Marwah-Wadwan area. Again, you know how neglected this sector has been at the hands of the Kashmir-centric tourism establishments.

"Horticulture will be our next thrust area. We can have apples from Mantalai and Bhaderwah, but we'll also have kiwis and olives from Ramban, pistachio from Doda, saffron from Kishtwar, pecan nut from Poonch, and mangoes, litchis, and kinoos from the Jammu-Udhampur-Kathua belt. Again, no Kashmiri Director of Horticulture will ever let us harness the full potential of our horticulture sector."

Monali nodded.

"Education will be our next industry. We already have so many BEd colleges. We can now have top-quality residential schools in places like Patnitop, and at least one medical hospital and colleges in each district, so that we have educational and medical tourism round-the-year."

"That's interesting," Monali said.

"Our biggest advantage is our manpower. They are educated and disciplined, unlike the Kashmiris who've just made stone pelting and hartals their biggest pastime."

Monali listened.

"We also love good infrastructure and have no problems if the army makes good roads for us. Unlike Kashmiris, we are not obsessed with religion, and not suspicious about anything coming from a non-co-religionist.

"We pay our electricity bills by the meter unlike Kashmiris. So, this sector will not be a black hole as it is now in Kashmir. We also pay 90% of the GST collected in the State, be it on industrial production, or liquor, or services. Also, the revenues from the Lakhanpur toll post, till it is wound up in accordance with the national norms, will accrue to us totally."

There was pin drop silence in the room.

"So, we have a very strong case for a separate State. Don't we Monaliji?" Sundal concluded.

Monali remained pensive for a moment. "Friends, you obviously realise that ... I'm no one to grant you Statehood. But I can only promise to take your demand to the appropriate quarters in the Government of India and hope for the best. Meanwhile, my request to you all would be to show restraint.

Please don't damage public property because then you'll have to repair these at your cost once you have your own State," smiled the Governor.

"Second, please keep on discussing the mechanics of running a separate State and please keep on identifying the team that will spearhead those efforts."

Monali got up to leave. "Let's end on this non-violent peaceful note for the time being," she said.

"One thing more, Your Excellency," the President of the Jammu Chamber of Commerce said, "what happens to our Jammu employees till then?"

"Their safety shall be ensured. And the Chief Secretary shall personally supervise that aspect."

"But will they be shifted to Jammu?"

"That option too is open, but let's wait and watch," Monali smiled as she marched off to her office.

* * *

The ADC escorted the Governor to her office, and mentioned, "Mam, the solar team from Delhi is waiting to see you. Should I usher them in?"

For a moment, Monali couldn't remember what the team had been called for. The huge implications of carving the Jammu Division from Kashmir were still swirling around her mind. "Oh, yes … I forgot. Yes, please send them in…. And Raj, I think you should just hold on for this meeting too."

"Any further instructions for me, Madam?" asked the Jammu DivCom.

"No, Suraj, you can leave. Just keep your eyes and ears open and let the Chief Secretary know if you hear anything funny."

* * *

The solar expert group from Delhi comprised four members. The Director Solar Energy Centre was the leader. There was one expert on appliance efficiencies, one on solar panel design, and the fourth on inverter and battery sizing.

As the group introduced itself, Monali introduced the Chief Secretary. She then started on the brief.

"Gentlemen, first let me thank you for being here at such a short notice. As you might know, we have a bit of an emergency here, which is that the J&K Government is unable to function in Srinagar. So, we have to make the Jammu Secretariat functional ASAP."

The team nodded.

"Now to do that, I want solar panels on the roof top of every building in the Jammu Secretariat – the main building, the annexe, the legislature, even the computer centre. In the second phase, if you deem fit, you can cover the parking areas too.

"Your inverter and battery expert should do the sizing in such a way that we first, make the Jammu Secretariat weatherproof, and second, make it export surplus energy to the grid through a two-way meter which I think you call net-meter.

"Your appliance efficiency expert, in parallel, should advise us on the cooling and heating devices that we need to keep our employees comfortable round-the-year. So, give me appropriately sized hot-and-cold inverter air conditioners, LED lighting, silver reflective glasses on the windows that reject heat but let in light, and so on.

"I find it strange that despite a solar revolution sweeping the rest of India, J&K is still maintaining its aloofness … which I suppose is linked with its DNA of separatist feelings. That is to change now … at least in Jammu.

"Now how fast can you do this?"

The Director SEC appeared to be shell-shocked.

"Mam," he stammered, "arranging funding, getting regulatory clearances, finalising tenders, selecting vendors, getting supplies, and installing them will take a minimum of er ... six months...."

"That is totally unacceptable," Monali snapped. "The maximum I may have is a week."

"Mam," Raj said, "let me co-ordinate this. Some parts, I'm sure, can be completed within a week. While the rest can be implemented over may be three months. Now, our priority is to make the employees somewhat comfortable. Which we can do by simply following the morning time-table of 7 am-2 pm that all field offices in Jammu in summer follow. In parallel, we can procure and install LED bulbs and inverter hot-and-cold air conditioners because these are generally on some government rate-contract or another. We can also get our PDD to strengthen the conventional electricity supply to the Secretariat so that we have some fool-proof back-up arrangements always.

"This should provide enough breathing time to the Director Saheb here to sort out the formalities for procuring and installing the solar PV system, and the inverters, and batteries, as you desire."

"Makes sense," the Governor nodded in agreement, "but that doesn't mean I'm relaxing my deadlines. This is war ... war against communal and anti-national elements. So, Director Saheb, please pull out all stops, and let's see what you can do for making the Jammu Secretariat the most energy-efficient government building in the country."

"Madam," said the Chief Secretary taking the hint that the meeting was over, "permit me please to take it from here....

And we assure you of showing some very positive results within a week."

With the delegation gone, Monali buzzed the ADC to get to the Prime Minister.

She also desired that the State aircraft be kept ready for a flight to Ladakh tomorrow morning.

That done, the Governor addressed the Chief Secretary, "Raj, you may find my obsession with solar energy a little whimsical, if not nonsensical."

As Raj looked on flabbergasted, she smiled, "But trust me. I'm talking from my own first-hand experience of having an 8-kVA solar power plant with 8 batteries, inverter, and a net-meter in my own house in Greater Noida. The lesson is, that if you can't tolerate even a second's disruption in your power supply, you need to have your own inverter, preferably a solar-connected inverter, based back-up ... because your grid-supply can be sabotaged. And I want this for Jammu Secretariat because this is going to be one big target for our very angry friends in Kashmir and Pakistan. Don't take this threat lightly, which I hope you won't, after your own experience at the hands of your own government."

"I get it, Mam," Raj nodded vigorously, "I'll personally review the security arrangements here, and will now insist on inverter-based CCTV monitoring and electrified fences in my plans. So that we are ready from tomorrow even while the solar panels take some time to reach us."

"That's the spirit," the Governor commented, "now what are you waiting for? Get hold of the DGP and the Power Secretary and get cracking."

* * *

The Prime Minister could call Monali back only a little later in the evening. He listened to her report about her interactions with the *Jammu Mukti Morcha* and appreciated her idea to now hold discussions with the Ladakhis.

"What about the Kargilis, however?" he asked.

"Sir, they generally wait and watch. Sometimes they respect 'Kashmiri sentiments', as they say, but most of the time they're quite reluctant to follow the Kashmiri diktats."

"Monaliji, there is no time now to request the Kargili leaders to join your meeting in Leh, as you know, they will take more than six hours to reach Leh. Also, for political reasons, and to assuage their egos that they are as important to us as the Leh leadership, it may be advisable to meet them in Kargil itself. So, I was wondering if it would be possible for you to make a brief halt in Kargil, on way to Leh, for just half-an-hour?" asked the Prime Minister.

"Certainly Sir, as you desire," assured the Governor.

"Great, then I will pass on instructions to let the Kargil leaders see you around 10 in Kargil Dak Bungalow. Bye Monaliji and wish you the best of luck."

"Good bye Sir," said Monali.

* * *

There was a flurry of activity as the security agencies contacted and sensitised Kargil leaders for the forthcoming interaction with the new Governor. The District Development Commissioner was asked to spruce up the Kargil Dak Bungalow. The police got cracking on the security and protocol *bandobast*. The Air Force was asked to keep the small airstrip in Kargil operational.

36

Ladakh, Saturday, 19 June 2021

BY 0940 hrs, watched over by a few sheep and goats, and the intrigued Pakistanis on the Kargil heights, the State plane had touched down at Kargil Airport. A journey that by road takes two days over some 500 kms of bone jarring surfaces was completed in about 30 minutes, thanks to modern technology, the Governor mused.

As Monali stepped out of the aircraft, a burning hot sun greeted her but the breeze was freezing cold. Typical climate of a cold desert, and what a drastic change from Jammu's 45-degree Celsius heat. She stared at the majestic snow-clad mountains and the bare landscape.

Dressed in an elegant turquoise blue silk saree paired with a matching blue blouse, the Governor was carrying a quilted down jacket in her hand – just in case the Ladakh weather took a turn for the worse. Walking a few steps made her a little out of breath. Monali realised she was in a high-altitude region, above 10,000 feet from mean sea level.

The Deputy Commissioner (DC) and Superintendent of Police (SP) were there to receive the Governor, but they left it to Mr Akhoon, the Chief Executive Councillor of the Ladakh Autonomous Hill Development Council, Kargil (LAHDC-K) to present the traditional white silk *khatak* garland to the Governor. That done, the delegation got into their designated cars, and moved to the meeting room in the DC's office complex.

Mr Akhoon introduced his fellow councillors, and gave a rousing welcome speech thanking the Governor to pay them a visit so soon after taking over as Governor, and *before she had been to Leh*. To good effect, he repeated the latter point thrice almost hinting that it was because of her that the Leh Council was being shown its place. He then dwelt on the harsh weather, the lack of electricity during winters, absentee teachers, ration shortage, unemployment among youth – in fact, everything except autonomy.

This public posturing was leading nowhere. So, the Governor thanked them all for their warm hospitality and desired to go to the Dak Bungalow. Separately, she called the DC and SP and instructed them to get all thirty councillors to meet her one by one.

To Mr Akhoon, she came straight to the point.

"Akhoon Saheb, you know very well what is happening in Kashmir and Jammu. So, I've come here to find out what exactly do you want – independence like Kashmir, separate Statehood like Jammu, or union territory status that has been the demand from Leh."

Akhoon was nonplussed. So, he hemmed and hawed. He talked of Kargil's business (and religious) ties with Kashmir and cultural affinities with Leh. He said it will be so difficult for Kargil as a State to survive on its own, cut-off as it was from the rest of the world for six months. Then there was

Pakistan constantly keeping them in the sights of its guns. In short, the status quo was the best option for Kargil.

"I get your point, Akhoon Saheb," Monali said, "but you know very well about the law-and-order situation in the Kashmir Valley currently. The State Government is unable to function there and we are very seriously thinking of operating from Jammu. So please tell me in case Kashmir breaks away from India, who would you like to go with? With independent Muslim Kashmir, or as a part of the Union Territory of Ladakh?"

Akhoon didn't know where to look. "Hmmm...."

Monali remained silent and expected Akhoon to say more.

"Hmmm ... I'd need to consult my colleagues over this 'hypothetical problem'."

The next Councillor was a little more forth right. He had no problem aligning with Kashmir in a united J&K. But if Kashmir were to break away, he thought the Shia Kargilis will be ill-treated. Pretty much the way Shias of Kashmir are treated by their Sunni brethren. A separate union territory status, therefore, was a preferable option.

The Councillor from the Buddhist region of Zanskar was the most clear-headed.

"Madam, Kashmiris ignore our infrastructure and developmental needs. Constantly. Our children feel very uncomfortable going for higher studies in Kargil or Kashmir. Where Islamic radical attitudes appear to be lurking just below the surface. You know of the perilous 4-5 day 'Chadar Trek' over the frozen Zanskar river? That our children have to undertake every spring to go to their schools in Leh? But what options do we have? Lately, thanks to the generosity of the Indian Air Force ... and thanks to their Siachen Pioneers helicopters ... some 40 kids get a lift to go to Leh from

Lingshed. So, Madam, we Zanskaris have no hesitation to admit that our fate is inextricably linked with Leh and – India. Please take us out of the clutches of both Kashmir and Kargil and merge us with Leh."

It was almost 1130, and the Kargilis still acted as confused as they were when the interactions had just begun. There was no point carrying on any further. So, Monali thanked them for their views and hospitality, and asked the ADC to get the State plane ready to take off for Leh.

* * *

By 1145 hours, the State plane was airborne, again. It circled over the green Suru Valley gaining height over the poplars, and the Khurbathang Plateau, headed towards the Fotu La Pass, then the Namika La Pass, over Lamayuru's moon land area, entered the Leh Valley, took a round of Leh town, and with the Spituk Monastery on its right, landed at the Kushok Bakula Rimpochee Airport Leh some 30 minutes later.

"Leh is a very popular airport nowadays, Mam," the Chief Secretary remarked looking at the two parked IndiGo and GoAir planes at the airport, "there are as many as 15 flights every day, I'm told."

"That's great," Monali said suitably impressed recalling those days some 35 years back when she was posted here and there used to be just four Indian Airlines flights a week.

Like Kargil, the Leh DC and SP were there to receive her and once again they let Dr Dawa, the Chief Executive Councillor of the Ladakh Autonomous Hill Development Council, Leh (LAHDC-L) to present the traditional white silk *khatak* garland to her. Monali recognised him almost immediately. He had worked with her some 35 years back. But now his front teeth were missing. He looked like he may have come from the age of the Pharaohs.

"Juley Madam," Dr Dawa said, "it's always a pleasure to welcome you back in Leh."

"Juley Dr Saheb," a beaming Monali replied, "but why have you become so old?"

"The pressures of the work ... and the high-altitude obviously," Dr Dawa guffawed, "but Mam, you look the same ... touch wood," and he touched his head as everyone laughed.

The welcome out of the way, the delegation once again got into their designated cars and moved to the meeting room in the DC's office complex.

"Madam," Dr Dawa asked, "it's almost lunch time. May we offer you some Tibetan Thupka soup or the Ladakhi *gur-gur* tea?"

"I'd have both Dr Saheb, but first the butter tea please."

"You know Raj," Monali said to the Chief Secretary, "I have personally always preferred the Ladakhi *gur-gur* tea over the Kashmiri *noon chai*. Both are made by boiling tea leaves in water for some time till the brew achieves a dark brown colour. In Ladakh, it is then skimmed, and poured into a cylinder with fresh yak butter and salt which is then shaken resulting in that typical *gur-gur* sound. The result is a purplish liquid which to me feels and tastes like soup. But in Kashmir, they put some baking soda too in the brew which makes it somewhat bitter, which I personally don't relish."

"Madam, you have described the process very well." Dr Dawa was impressed. "Except that the demand here is so much that we now have to use Amul butter in place of yak butter. That affects the flavour somewhat."

Flavour or stink? the DGP thought but kept it to himself.

"Madam," the Chief Executive Councillor said, "May I introduce my colleagues?" and proceeded to introduce all 29 of them. That took some time while the *gur-gur* tea was served.

Then he began, “Madam, our stand has been crystal clear from the time this Council came into existence in 1995. And that is – we want complete freedom from Kashmir, and the communal and anti-national policies they believe in.

“But our problem is that we are so damn land-locked. Cut-off for over six months in a year from the world as the Zozilla Pass on the Kashmir side and the Barlacha La and Rohtang passes on the Manali side get blocked with as much as sixty feet of snow. The tunnelling work that the Government of India has so very kindly started on all these passes is unfortunately yet to gather speed and so we apprehend no change in our situation for the next 3-4 years.

“But even when the tunnels are commissioned, we will still have a very short agricultural season and will never be able to grow staples like rice or wheat. Ever. It will be barley and vegetables then for us for quite some time. Fortunately … thanks to the Army we have a ready market for our vegetables and fruits right here in Leh. Otherwise the Kashmiris had totally sabotaged this sector by alleging that our produce suffered from some er … the Codling Moth disease, which we contest vehemently, but to no avail.

“Our tourism sector is booming, thanks to world famous films, like 3 Idiots … you know Madam, which were shot here. Also, the impression that unlike Kashmir there are no terrorists here has helped us. Even our border areas adjoining Pakistan and China are much quieter and so tourists can go fearlessly even in the Nubra and Pangong Lake areas. But this season too is limited to only 3-4 months in the summers.

“Our population is still around 1,50,000 and even if Kargil joins us, it will not exceed 3,00,000. That by any standard is a tiny base for any taxation exercise. Which means – we will forever depend on the generosity of the Government of India and that’s why we have very coolly and rationally decided that unlike Jammu we will not ask for Statehood but only a union territory status. Like you have for Lakshadweep, Andaman-Nicobar, or Puducherry. May be in due course, we would try to attain full Statehood as Goa has.

"And Madam, it may be politically imprudent to admit but the truth as you know very well is, that we Ladakhis hate Kashmiris ... from the bottom of our heart. They have always exploited us economically and denied us our basic economic and political rights. They have tried to kill our agriculture, horticulture, and handicrafts sector but with Buddha's grace haven't succeeded. But what is unbearable now is the way they have tried to spoil our tourism sector by exporting jihadists. That is now the proverbial final straw on the camel's back.

"So, Madam Governor, that's in brief our case for getting the union territory status and for seceding from Kashmir. And unlike the Kargilis, every Buddhist living anywhere in Ladakh is unanimous in wanting this status."

"Thank you, Dr Saheb," Monali said, "for this excellent introduction. But you have said nothing about the energy situation here. Can you be self-sufficient on that front, ever?"

"Madam," Dr Dawa said, "we do have decent hydro resources that we're ready to let the NHPC or the private sector exploit, but the lead times are immense and our harsh winters reduce all their capacities by almost 80%. Solar is the answer, but that is so expensive. Also, the batteries remain the weakest link there till we have some breakthrough.

"We do have geothermal springs in Puga, Chumathang, etc but the temperatures are not high enough for generating electricity. Experts tell us that we can use that heat for green houses or tourist spas but we are still working out the implications of acting on that advice.

"So, we can't have self-sufficiency in energy but that doesn't mean we have to be dependent on Kashmir for any of our needs here. Most of what we need can very well come from the Manali route, which is the shortest way to get to us from Northern India."

"I get your point, Dr Dawa," nodded Monali, "but tell me your views about opening the Kailash-Mansarovar route."

"Madam," Dr Dawa's eyes glistened in excitement, "you get that and then we will be economically self-sufficient too. This is the only idea that can get us tourists in winter. And trade with China all the year round."

"Currently pilgrims wishing to go to Kailash-Mansarovar have to cross the Lipulekh Pass in Uttarakhand after trekking over a treacherous terrain for almost a month. This restricts the yatra to only the young and the physically fit. There are horrendous logistical challenges too on this route. With avalanches, landslides, and medical problems adding to the complexity of the entire operation.

"Compared to that, there is no trek at all if you go to Kailash-Mansarovar from Leh. There is a 500-kilometre or so road journey one-way. But the roads are excellent. So, a pilgrim can take a flight from Delhi and reach Leh in an hour. Then acclimatise for two days enjoying the sights and sounds and cuisine of Leh. And then take a vehicle, cross Demchok in Nyoma area and reach Kailash-Mansarovar in just two days.

"And technically, they can go on this route all-around the year, because there are no avalanches on the way. There is no snow either as it is all a cold, arid desert."

There was pin-drop silence in the Conference Room as the implications of opening this route dawned on everyone.

"So where are we on this proposal?" Monali asked.

"Madam," the Chief Secretary said, "I have seen the files and understand it is still stuck with the China Desk in the Ministry of External Affairs in Delhi."

"Okay," Monali nodded, "let me see if I can do something."

"Let's then break for lunch on this very exciting note," Dr Dawa said as he rose to escort the Governor to a small dining table.

The table had formal seating for just four dignitaries: The Governor, Chief Secretary, DGP, and the Chief Executive Councillor. All other guests had to serve themselves from a long table on which an elaborate buffet was laid out.

"Madam, we have sent food for the pilot and co-pilot of the State aircraft to the airport," Dr Dawa said.

"That's nice," Monali said, "and I hope our drivers and security personnel too are being looked after."

"You don't have to worry Madam," Dr Dawa replied, "They are all our guests today."

The first course of Thupka, the Tibetan soup with noodles and veggies, was served almost immediately. That alone would have sufficed, but Dr Dawa couldn't even countenance the possibility. So, you had momos, kothas (which is fried momos), chicken chilly, fried rice, seasonal vegetables like cauliflower and cabbage, and even a mutton roganjosh. For dessert, tinned rasgollas were served, thanks obviously to the nearest Army Canteen.

"Raj," Monali addressed the Chief Secretary, "before we return to Srinagar, I'd like to meet the GOC XIV Corps and the IG ITBP. I believe my office has already sensitised them; so please just confirm that I'll be able to see them after half an hour, say by 1430 hrs."

Lunch done, Monali was escorted to the VVIP Guest House, where she met the GOC and the ITBP Commander. Both assured they were ready to open the Kailash-Mansarovar route if that was what the government desired. They also thought that there would be no great resistance from the Chinese side to this proposal.

Before the meeting ended, the ITBP Commander handed over a satellite phone to Monali.

"Madam, our DG in Delhi has asked me to hand this over to you as there is an important call coming for you soon."

Monali knew what that meant and kept the set on the side table. Sure enough, just 15 minutes later, the phone rang, and it was the PMO on the other side.

"Good afternoon Madam, if you could just hold for a minute … the Prime Minister will like to speak to you."

The Governor indicated with her eyes to everyone to vacate the room, just when the familiar voice crackled on the other end.

"Monaliji, I hope you had a great meeting in Kargil and Leh."

"Oh, yes Sir," and she went on to give the full report. "And now Sir, as you had desired, we have to give our full attention to *Operation Mansarovar*."

"Yes, Monaliji," the Prime Minister said. "And that's why we're having the Chinese Foreign Minister this Monday, which is … 21 June, day-after-tomorrow. I'd very much like you to be there. We will, of course, discuss the other plans that you may have for Jammu and Ladakh thereafter. Like Operation Manali?"

"As you desire, Sir, I'd be there."

"See you then Monaliji, and God bless you."

"Good day, Sir," as the call disconnected.

37

Srinagar, Saturday, 19 June 2021

THE Governor could land in Srinagar only by 1630 hrs and be in Raj Bhavan by 1700 hrs.

"Madam, the situation is still volatile," the DGP had briefed her. "In fact, the Hurriyat has warned that if we shift the Secretariat to Jammu, there will be rivers-of-blood on the streets in Kashmir."

Monali stared at the DGP with steel in her eyes.

"Okay, then let's call their bluff, and let's shift tomorrow, on a Sunday. And we start operating in Jammu after a week from next Monday, which would be…."

"28 June Madam," the Chief Secretary suggested.

"That's right, Raj."

The Jammu staff was readying itself since June 17, the day the Governor had hinted at the possibility of shifting them to Jammu. But full move? With all files, computers, and trunks? That was an operation that usually took a month, Raj thought.

But orders were orders. And secretly, even Kashmiris were happy to escape the daily tyranny of the Hurriyat on the roads even when you were hale and hearty. Because only God could help you if you fell sick.

So, what the heck? We have had so many experiments in this blasted State. Let's have one more.

"We will move day-after-tomorrow, Madam as you ordered," Raj said as he took out his notebook to jot down the points needed to make this mammoth task a success.

"And Raj," Monali added, "facilitate the move of every central agency that would also like to shift to Jammu. For example, the offices of the Auditor General, the Post Master General, the Income Tax Commissioner, Passport Officer … and anyone you can think of. They can be much more productive in Jammu … unless they too have some Kashmiri employees who would prefer twiddling their thumbs here."

* * *

Sunday, June 20, 2021

The SRTC and JKTDC buses filled to the brim with Jammu employees started moving at 0400 hrs on June 20, 2021 as scheduled. They were warned not to sing or raise slogans while in the Valley and were happy to comply.

Before the Hurriyat guys woke up, the convoys were crossing the Banihal tunnel and stopping for their first break at the Banihal Dak Bungalow.

In parallel, the records were being shifted by the JKP and CRPF jawans under the able supervision of some valiant Kashmiri officers who had toiled the whole night to see that the last file in the Secretariat was safely packed and loaded.

The first news about the operation came out in the newspapers on Monday morning. By then, the trucks were in Jammu and were being unloaded by the Jammu employees.

And Monali had landed in Delhi.

* * *

The news of the Secretariat move spread like wild fire in Kashmir. The Hurriyat gathered a crowd and declared *Jihad*. Mobs threw stones at policemen and set fire to the Tourist Reception Centre (TRC) because that was where Jammu employees had once stayed. Luckily, the building was almost empty as the employees had already shifted to Jammu.

The smoke rose in such heavy columns that you could spot it from miles away. The fire brigade was called to douse the fire. But it was too late. This was the second time the TRC had been burnt down, the first one being in 2004 when the bus service to Muzaffarabad was launched by Shri Atal Bihari Vajpayee, the then Prime Minister.

Angry mobs on the directions of Hurriyat even set fire to some JKTDC buses which had allegedly transported some employees to Jammu.

38

Delhi, Monday, 21 June 2021

THE scheduled meeting with the Chinese Foreign Minister was at 1130 hrs but suddenly the PM wanted to have a briefing session at 1000.

"Any last-minute doubts, please clear now," he had requested. And that was the cue for Soniji, the External Affairs Minister to start off.

"Sir, from day one, our opposition to opening the Leh route for the Kailash-Mansarovar yatra has been consistent. We are against this proposal primarily because it forces us to open an immigration check-point in Demchok-Nyoma, which we apprehend will legitimatise the Chinese illegal occupation of the Aksai Chin area and dilute considerably our just claims thereon.

"Second, because huge number of pilgrims are expected to go on this route, the External Affairs Ministry will have to deploy more personnel to process their immigration cases. That will undoubtedly put a heavy burden on our limited resources as it will be impossible to arrange staff that is acclimatised to function in this cold and high-altitude area.

"Third, no route can remain one-way. And so sooner than later, the Chinese will like to trade through this route which will again increase the burden on our personnel considerably.

"Fourth, this route will harm the current yatra through Uttarakhand, which will affect adversely the rural economy of the Pithoragarh region. This has been conveyed to me by the CM there, personally."

The Foreign Minister took a brief pause. "So, Patel Bhai, although we know we have to clear this proposal in national interest, we in the External Affairs Ministry remain very uncomfortable about the whole idea."

"Thank you Soniji for highlighting your concerns again," the Prime Minister said. "Earlier, we have had similar inputs from the Defence and Home Ministries, who too were initially hesitant, but they are mostly on-board now. Now the J&K Governor has just been to Ladakh, and I'd very much like to have her assessment from the field."

The PM turned towards Monali. "So Monaliji, what's your advice?"

"Thank you, Sir, for inviting me to this very important meeting," Monali began. "My support for opening this route stems from just two reasons. First, that it will save lives – of countless Hindu pilgrims who are dying rather unnecessarily because of the hardships on the current Pithoragarh-Lipulekh route.

"Second, it will boost Ladakh's economy like nothing can. And that in due course will extend to every hamlet that falls on the Manali-Leh route. The Government of India will have to upgrade roads, and build tunnels, and even railway lines on this route but I'm sure this all will be quite worth the effort."

Monali paused and looked at Soniji. Soniji's face had turned stern hinting that she wasn't liking this even one bit. "Coming to the External Affairs Ministry's objections," Monali continued, "I understand that their employees will be quite reluctant to serve at Demchok at around 14,000 feet altitude in freezing conditions that last for almost nine months in a year. But I see in that predicament a great opportunity to employ local Ladakhis, who could initially come on deputation from the Police, Ladakh Scouts, ITBP, and so many other organisations posted in the Ladakh region. I've no doubt that these superbly acclimatised personnel can after a little training do the job as well as the Delhi Police personnel who currently man the immigration counters at the Indira Gandhi International Airport.

"As for trade, that is actually a very good idea. Already there is a lot of smuggling going on as you can see from the kind of Chinese pottery and toys and blankets flooding the Leh market. Some pashmina also comes in which I think is a good thing for the shawl weavers and embroiderers in Kashmir. Since Chinese supply lines are a little stretched in this region, I see a great potential for food grains and vegetables going from our side to China which will fetch better prices for our farmers in Ladakh, Himachal Pradesh, and even Punjab. In the long run, I think that will be great for our farmers everywhere. And in turn, if the Chinese send in more crockery or electronic goods, our customs should deal with them in the same manner as they deal with them elsewhere in the country.

"As for the objections of the Uttarakhand Government, I am not suggesting that we totally abandon the Lipulekh route. We can still use it for people who are younger, fitter, and more adventurous and who wish to rough it out on this particular route to Kailash-Mansarovar. But we should have some empathy for the old and the infirm who could be quite content to take the motorable route via Leh."

Monali noticed that many in the room were nodding in silent support. Good news! "So, Sir, if the Defence and the Home Ministries are already on-board, we would request the blessings of the External Affairs Ministry too. This is a revolutionary … dream project for the inhabitants of Leh, Kargil, Zanskar, and the Lahaul-Spiti areas because once pilgrims complete their yatras, they would certainly like to visit all other areas of tourist interest in these regions which have been popularised by so many Hindi films like *3 Idiots*.

"And if trade also starts on this route, it will have such a force-multiplier effect on this region's economy, agriculture, and employment that we can't even imagine."

Monali paused, carefully choosing her words. "So … Sir, I'm really excited about the potential for opening the Leh route for Kailash-Mansarovar and would request all agencies of the government to go all out to support this idea."

There was pin-drop silence in the room as all present reflected on the picture that the J&K Governor was projecting.

"That does it then," the Prime Minister said, "let's now proceed for our lunch with the Chinese."

* * *

The official banquet was at the Durbar Hall of the Government of India's 5-star Hotel Ashok. Zhu, the Chinese Foreign Minister floored the Indians with his clipped English, and *propuh* British manners. No substitution of the 'R' sound by the 'L', and no sing-song accent at all.

"He was an Oxford don after all," someone whispered in the PM's ears.

The Chinese ambassador on the other hand was trying to converse in Hindi which was impressive and hilarious at the same time.

There was so much bonhomie all-around that Monali couldn't believe that this was the same country which was supposed to be swallowing us since the 1962 war.

The document-signing ceremony for opening the Leh route for the Kailash-Mansarovar yatra between the Chinese and Indian Foreign Ministers was a breeze. As cameras clicked and flash bulbs blinded the dignitaries, the Prime Minister along with the Defence Minister, Home Minister, and the J&K Governor clapped enthusiastically.

The devil will be in the details, but for the time being no one resented at history being made.

39

Delhi, Tuesday, 22 June 2021

"MONALIJI, can you stay on in Delhi for a day longer? I have one more important matter to discuss."

The Prime Minister had desired when the dinner with the Chinese Foreign Minister was over.

So here was the J&K Governor at 7 Race Course Road, now Lok Kalyan Road, the official residence of the Indian Prime Minister sharp at 0900 hrs on Tuesday, June 22, 2021.

"The Prime Minister will just join you, Madam," the Private Secretary to the PM said as he ushered Monali to the conference room.

There were three, or four, officers already waiting in the conference table. They got up and greeted as Monali came in.

"Ah, the usual gang of four," Monali smiled as she could place the Cabinet Secretary, the Principal Secretary to the PM, the Home Secretary, and the Law Secretary.

"Madam, we have had to bother you because we needed your inputs on this important legal matter," said the Cabinet Secretary as he passed on a folder marked 'TOP SECRET' to the Governor.

As Monali took a seat next to the PM's chair, and opened the folder, the words 'Jammu and Kashmir Reorganisation Act, 2021' jumped at her. More or less, modelled after the 'Andhra Pradesh Reorganisation Act, 2014', this was to be an Act of the Indian Parliament. When passed, it would trifurcate the State of Jammu and Kashmir into Jammu, Kashmir, and the Union Territory of Ladakh.

"Pardon me," Monali said, "but wasn't the bill rejected by the J&K Assembly in its winter session last year?"

"Yes, it was Monaliji." The voice sounded different this time. Like the PM's. Monali turned her head towards the door and saw that the Prime Minister had entered the conference room. "But that is a legal problem the Law Secretary will explain." The PM looked towards the Law Secretary. "Sharmaji, if you would care to...."

As everyone got up to greet the PM that was the cue the learned Law Secretary was waiting for. So, he explained how way back in 2014 the then *Andhra Pradesh Reorganisation Act, 2013*, was rejected by the Andhra Pradesh Legislative Assembly on 30 January 2014. Then he quoted Article 3 of the Constitution of India 1949 that stipulated that Parliament may by law:

(a) *form a new State by separation of territory from any State or by uniting two or more States or parts of States or by uniting any territory to a part of any State;*
(b) *increase the area of any State;*
(c) *diminish the area of any State;*
(d) *alter the boundaries of any State;*
(e) *alter the name of any State;*

Provided that no Bill for the purpose shall be introduced in either House of Parliament except on the recommendation of the President and unless, where the proposal contained in the Bill affects the area, boundaries or name of any of the States, the Bill has been referred by the President **to the Legislature of that State for expressing its views thereon** *within such period as may be specified in the reference or within such further period as the President may allow and the period so specified or allowed has expired.*

The Law Secretary next narrated the cases in the Honourable Supreme Court that had commented on the validity of these provisions. And underlined, that what has been settled is that the Legislature of the affected State is only required to 'express its views' which the President of India may, or may not, agree with.

That's why, even when the Andhra Pradesh Legislative Assembly voted to reject its proposed split, the Parliament of India ignored those 'views' and went ahead carving out a separate State of Telangana with Hyderabad as the capital of both States for ten years.

"So Monaliji," the PM clarified, "it doesn't really matter whether J&K agrees with this proposed Act or not. What I want – is your views on its timing. Tell me the approximate date from which this Act should come in force and we will accordingly work backwards to pass it in the Parliament here."

"And Sir," Monali replied, "the violence in Kashmir that this Act would unleash would not be a constraint, I suppose."

"Kashmiris will be violent Monaliji ... that's a given, whether or not we do anything. But as a responsible government, we can't keep the people of Jammu and Ladakh a hostage of the so called Kashmiri sentiments, anymore," the PM said. The steeliness of his tone startled Monali.

"In that case Sir," Monali replied, "we should do this all before the durbar move at the end of October 2021. That would ensure that Kashmiris ... officials and politicians ... don't have to shift to Jammu this winter, which in turn will free a lot of office and residential accommodation for the Jammu staff and make our planning for a new State somewhat easier."

Everyone was silent for a few moments. As the PM looked towards the Cabinet Secretary, Sanjeev replied, "Sir, we will still have time to process things here. But I suppose the Honourable Minister for Parliamentary Affairs can shed more light on the mechanics involved."

"I'll sensitise him personally. Any other formalities?" the PM said.

"Yes Sir," the Law Secretary said, "we need to put a date from which this Act will come in effect."

"Monaliji, any views?" the PM asked.

"Sir, in that case let us put 1 October 2021 ... or wait...." Monali checked the calendar on her mobile, "7 October is better as it is the start of winter Navratras. That will be quite an auspicious date for Jammuwallas."

"7 October 2021 is the date then. Let's work backwards and ensure everything is taken care of in the time we have from now till 6 October 2021," the PM declared as he got up signalling the end of the meeting.

"Madam, the project still remains TOP SECRET till the matter is moved in the Parliament," the Cabinet Secretary said.

"I understand," Monali nodded.

"And Madam, I suppose you are fine with the boundaries proposed for Jammu," the Cabinet Secretary asked.

"I noticed you are converting the geographical boundaries of the existing Jammu Division into a separate State, which is not what the Kashmiris want.... Their plan was to treat the river Chenab as a border, and consequently retain Banihal,

Doda etc with them. But administratively, I agree with your logic more."

"That settles it then, Mam. Anything else, gentlemen," the CabSec asked.

"Madam, we have to also get cracking on the list of paid agents of Kashmiri political parties in Kishtwar, Doda, Banihal, Rajouri, and Poonch so that they are all rounded up around the 1st of October 2021," the Home Secretary suggested.

"That will be helpful," Monali said.

There were suggestions on moving Hindu artefacts from Kashmir Museums to Jammu, lest they be destroyed by angry mobs in Kashmir, Bamiyan style ... on splitting the bureaucracy between the two States ... of dividing treasuries ... of determining the share in electricity from projects in both regions ... of splitting the interest burden between the two States....

The Cabinet Secretary had a full check-list running into several pages that he shared a copy with the Governor.

"I know Mam," the Cabinet Secretary smiled, "all this can't be finished by the D-date, but I thought you should know the full drill."

40

Srinagar, 15 September 2021

LIFE continued as expected. Every Friday remained a day of violent protests in Kashmir. Why Friday? Because every Friday Muslims are supposed to pray with their community in a mosque. For terrorists, that presents an excellent opportunity to arouse the passions of a captive audience and to exhort them to throw stones at the infidels (meaning Indians) after the prayers. In the process, if the belief that Islam is a religion of peace is belied, so be it!

Jammu was peaceful by and large, except for a "Separate Jammu from Kashmir" march every Monday.

Why Monday? Because Monday is called *Somvar* in Hindi where *Som* stands for the Moon god. It is said that at Somnath in Gujarat, *Som* (Moon) had prayed to Lord Shiva for thousands of years; where after Lord Shiva agreed to adorn him on his head. And had announced that anyone praying to him (Lord Shiva) on a Monday will earn merit.

Ladakhis would be mostly quiet till a Kashmiri taxi would straggle into Leh. Slogans of making Ladakh a union territory would then erupt from every lane forcing the Kashmiri taxi to double back to Srinagar, without carrying back any passenger!

Came 14 September 2021, and it was time to begin 'Operation Hasina'.

The ex-CM was holidaying in Dubai, or rather looking after her properties in the UAE, when she received word that Government of India was considering 'restoring popular rule' in J&K. So, if she could please rush back....

Which she did with alacrity.

"Is it true, Monaliji ... that you are revoking Governor's Rule soon," Hasina asked anxiously; when she met the Governor on 15 September 2021 in the Srinagar Raj Bhavan.

"That depends," Monali smiled, "on whether you and your party are willing to restore peace in the Valley."

"That we can sure try," Hasina replied, "but with what face would I go to my people?"

"Why? Just say that you have forced Government of India to bend down and recognise your undisputed leadership in J&K."

"No ... No, Monaliji," Hasina said, "that is not enough. I have to go with something that I have snatched away from Government of India. Like...."

Monali waited.

"Like ... getting the Uri project from NHPC," Hasina blurted out.

"Okay," Monali replied, "maybe I can arrange that."

"Getting the Army to vacate Tattoo Ground in Srinagar, and similar occupations in Gulmarg, Baramulla, Pattan...."

"I'll try," Monali replied.

"And scrapping the Indus Water Treaty?"

"No, that won't be possible … because that's an international matter with the World Bank also as a party," Monali narrowed her eyes.

"Having my own person as Chief Secretary?"

"Agreed, but after 15 days?"

"Agreed." Hasina beamed and shook hands with Monali warmly.

* * *

A brief ceremony was held on the lawns of the Srinagar Raj Bhavan. Hasina Ittoo with her old Kashmiri Cabinet Ministers took the oath of office and secrecy. Her Jammu colleagues refused to attend claiming they were now fully focused on their dream of establishing Jammu as a separate State.

Hasina flew to Jammu the next day to persuade the Secretariat employees in Jammu to come back to Srinagar. But a 10,000-strong crowd didn't allow her to even step out of the Jammu Airport. Dejected, and fuming, she returned to Srinagar with only the top brass comprising the Chief Secretary, Home Secretary, DGP, and the Finance Secretary accompanying her.

NHPC agreed to hand over the Uri and the Kishanganga projects. That was the big news of the day. Hasina claimed it as a huge political victory *where the Indian colonial and exploitative mindset was subjugated by the Kashmiri sentiment of Azaadi*. The fine print of the transfer agreement, however, stipulated that NHPC employees will continue to run the hydro projects till 31 March 2022, or for six more months, for which charges at the current rates shall be debited to the revenues of the project. NHPC was also authorised to withhold remittance of any revenues to the State till it recovered fully the depreciated value of the structures, equipment, and the compensation for the land that the project had paid for.

Army handed over Tattoo Ground in Srinagar to the State Government. They also promised to shift HAWS (The High-Altitude Warfare School) from Gulmarg to Baltal, near Sonemarg, by 31 March 2022. For all other properties, they said they will revert soon.

Hasina let the Secretariat run at Jammu as after a month she also had to move to Jammu in any case.

41

Srinagar, 7 October 2021

HASINA was stunned. Sadiq Karra, her MP in Delhi had informed her that the Monsoon session of the Indian Parliament that normally gets over by the end of September, was being extended by a week to pass the much dreaded 'Jammu and Kashmir Reorganisation Bill 2021'.

"Can they really do that?" Hasina was incredulous, "when we, the State Government, have not cleared that?"

"Yes Hasinaji," Sadiq clarified, "they claim they can. Under rules, they have to *consult* you, ONLY, which they apparently have."

"Karra Saheb, then move heaven and earth to see that this Bill doesn't go through."

The sessions in both the houses of the Parliament were stormy. Most opposition parties staged walk outs – several times. All MPs of Hasina's party gave long speeches and opposed stridently the 'Jammu and Kashmir Reorganisation

Act 2021'. Some fringe groups like the Muslim Independent Majlis of Hyderabad supported them by throwing out papers and mikes in the Parliament.

But with the brute majority that the Bharatiya Independent Party of the PM had, the Bill was passed on the seventh and the last day of the Monsoon Session. It received the assent of the President of India soon thereafter and came into operation from 7 October 2021 making Jammu the 30th State of the Indian Union, and Ladakh the 8th Union Territory of India.

Simultaneously, the Indian Parliament invoked its constituent powers under Article 368(1) of the Indian Constitution to abolish "Article 370: Temporary provisions with respect to the State of Jammu and Kashmir." The ground: the provision was 'temporary' to start with; and secondly, there was no justification to retain it once the 'State of Jammu and Kashmir' itself ceased to exist.

Hasina's MPs fought tooth and nail against the abolition of Article 370 which they claimed was a 'bridge' between India and J&K. They argued that if this bridge went down, so would the constitutional relationship they had with India. But it looked like the BIP couldn't care less.

Kashmir observed hartals, and black days for the entire duration the two matters were debated in the Parliament. But Jammu and Ladakh remained in a huge celebratory mood.

* * *

Hasina demanded to see the Prime Minister but couldn't get an appointment. She, along with Graboo the Finance Minister, then called on the Governor and were immediately ushered in.

"Monaliji," Hasina was furious, "what kind of game this Hindu fundamentalist party in Delhi wants to play with us? Kashmir has always been an international dispute, and you solve that by cutting Jammu and Ladakh away from us?"

"Hasinaji," Monali was all sugar-and-honey, "it's all political, you know very well. There is nothing to be taken personally. Your party should have managed Jammu and Ladakh better, I suppose...."

"No, no, no ... this is not a failure of our party cadre but a total manipulation of separatist and communal sentiments by the BJP. But tell me, Monaliji, even if they ... the Indian Government ... had to form a separate Jammu State, why could they not follow the Chenab line? How can the Muslim-majority areas of Doda, Ramban, Poonch, and Rajouri be forced to live with a Hindu Jammu? If Delhi wanted a separate State for Jammu, it should have constituted it with just the two-and-a-half districts of Jammu, Kathua, and Udhampur where Hindus live."

"But Hasinaji," Monali countered, "States in India are formed on either linguistic or administrative considerations. And never on communal lines. India can never agree to make another Pakistan. Because in Pakistan too, look what happened? The Bengali speaking Muslims separated from the Punjabi speaking Muslims. And there are now movements for a separate Baluchistan for Baluch Muslims, Pakhtoonistan for Pakhtoon Muslims, Sindh for Sindhi-speaking Muslims and what not. Even internationally, Muslims don't live in one big continent but are spread over some 57 countries. So, what's wrong if for Jammu, Kashmir, and Ladakh too linguistic and administrative considerations have prevailed?"

"Monaliji, but what happens to the international dimensions of the J&K dispute?"

"I'd let that be handled by the External Affairs Ministry in Delhi. I or you can't do much about any international matter." Monali took a deliberate pause. "Can we?"

"Monaliji, this all is so upsetting. Instead of Jammu and Kashmir, we just have a moth-eaten Kashmir.... Just like

Jinnah was duped into having a moth-eaten Pakistan. How would we survive financially?"

Monali grinned. Hasina had finally come to the crucial point. In fact, the most crucial point. Financial independence.

"But Hasinaji, I thought you were all ready to wrest full independence from India. What would have happened to your finances then?... Right now, you will continue to have your special status ... your normal share of funds from the central kitty, provided, of course, that you allow the collection of your share of GST and income tax from Kashmiri businessmen. You still have full control over your tourism, horticulture, and handicrafts sectors without feeling guilty about balancing Jammu's or Ladakh's needs in those sectors ... you can really become Asia's Switzerland that you always wanted to be ... without the debilitating, as you say, baggage of Jammu and Ladakh...."

"Monaliji, as an old J&K cadre person, you know very well what I'm hinting at. My problem is how do I pay my employees' salaries this month...?" Hasina's voice had a genuine concern. "My income has been cut by 70%, but I still have to pay 80% of the salaries ... because 80% of our employees, you know, are from Kashmir."

"Hasinaji, again ... this problem was always there ... when all your agencies were giving preference to recruiting more and more people from Kashmir. As to what you can do now, I understand there is a committee of senior officers looking into all cases of fraudulent recruitments ... you know where recruitments have taken place without sanctions, and in violation of all recruitment norms. You can immediately act on that report and terminate the services of all such persons," the Governor suggested.

"And send all those thousands to the streets to pelt stones at us?" Hasina was furious. "Come on, Monaliji, this suggestion is not practicable at all."

"Then make those employees more productive … by shifting them to public sector units … or to new public-private partnership ventures…."

"Monaliji, you too know very well that most of these employees have been recruited to cook food at the residence of officers. So, you really think they can be redeployed to do anything else … for those fancy public-private partnership ventures, as you suggest?"

Monali shrugged. "Then Hasinaji, what's the way out? Jammu and Ladakh are not going to come back to your fold. You thought all those Muslim-majority areas of Kargil, Doda, Poonch, or Rajouri will clamour to join Kashmir. But that too has not happened. So, tell me frankly, what is the solution to the financial emergency – that you think you will soon face?"

"The Central Government has to bail us out … what else?" Graboo intervened, "As they always have?"

Monali remained silent for a moment. "Let me communicate that to the Government of India … and you can continue with all those cooks till then, I suppose."

Hasina glared at the apparent sarcasm, but Monali kept a straight face with not even a hint of a smirk, smile … anything.

"Madam Governor," Graboo intervened again, "we will have to raise taxes. For example, if we levy a tax of ₹ 1,000 or so on every tourist who comes to Kashmir –"

"Shut up Graboo Saheb," Hasina retorted. "Who is coming to Kashmir nowadays with all the stone peltings, and hartals, and terrorist, sorry militant, strikes here? And you want to tax even the few who wish to come."

"No, Hasinaji," Graboo was in no mood to give up, "there is a certain category of tourists who will come regardless of the disturbed conditions here."

Hasina blinked. "And pray, who are they?"

"The Amarnath pilgrims," Graboo announced triumphantly, "why one thousand, we could charge them ₹ 10,000 each and they will still come."

"Don't be so sure Graboo Saheb," Monali smiled, "if you try to create difficulties here, pilgrims can very easily patronise some other route. For example, through Minamarg, in Kargil, I'm told. Or, go for the Kailash-Mansarovar yatra which route is now open via Leh. Muslims may be obliged to perform Haj in a particular geographical area of Saudi Arabia. But as you know Hindus ... how do I put it ... like to pick-and-choose from a bigger menu of holy sites."

"Enough on tourists and pilgrims, Graboo Saheb," Hasina barked, "let's focus on how will we all survive the winters here? We were all so used to going to the warmer climes of Jammu every winter."

"Time to go back to your Turkish Hammams then Hasinaji, which you claim make Kashmir winters much more pleasurable than the Jammu ones," Monali asked.

"I still stand by that sentiment, but what do we do for our offices? Electric heating is the only way out and how will we buy power when no one pays here for electricity?" Hasina lamented.

"Think about it, Hasinaji," Monali smiled as she got up, "and do let me know how I can be of any help. Now if you could kindly excuse me, I have to attend to some urgent matters ... now."

* * *

The Pakistani Army shelled the border areas of Jammu relentlessly. Pakistan also moved the UN to claim that India was altering illegally the boundaries of the disputed State of Jammu and Kashmir. India struck back by quoting how Pakistan had already given away a huge chunk of the same 'disputed territory' to China for its Karakoram Highway project.

Monali continued as the Governor for both Jammu and Kashmir, and Lieutenant Governor for the Union Territory of Ladakh. Mr Sundal and Dr Dawa became the first Chief Ministers of the Interim Governments of Jammu and Ladakh respectively till elections could be held.

The opening date for the Rohtang and Barlacha La tunnels on the Rohtang route was advanced to 30 November 2021 and the Prime Minister himself flew in to flag off traffic on this route. For the first time in history, trucks plied on this route all winter. There was no news, however, of the commissioning date of the Zozila tunnel.

In Kashmir, Hasina Ittoo remained in power. With Fukhtoo as her Chief Secretary. All charges had been dropped against Fukhtoo. No one could prove that he had sexually exploited girls in exchange for government jobs, as the witnesses, who had been *compensated adequately* had *turned hostile* in court.

Jammu dismantled the Lakhanpur toll post in accordance with the latest GST norms, while Kashmir erected a new one at Qazigund. That made goods in Kashmir twenty percent more expensive than they were in Jammu.

The move also opened up dozens of smuggling routes all over the Pir Panjal ranges with Gujjar-Bakarwals (the nomads), helping to smuggle all kinds of items of daily use to Kashmir.

Hasina threatened a *Poori Azaadi* (complete freedom) movement. Hurriyat happily joined in. Pakistan promised its full 'moral support' to the idea.

Pakistan also ordered the training of two fidayeen squads for Jammu – one to target its Secretariat, and another the Holy Shrine of Vaishno Devi.

42

Srinagar, Friday, 31 December 2021

THIS was the worst New Year eve party that Lieutenant General Gurdial Singh Sandhu, the Corps Commander of 15 Corps of the Indian Army, had ever attended in his distinguished army career of almost 38 years. The mood was sober, nay sombre. Everyone was nursing a glass of whiskey, beer, or whatever was their poison that evening, but their thoughts lay elsewhere.

The packing up was more heart-breaking, than back-breaking, to say the least. Every two years, officers and soldiers of the Indian Army had to re-locate themselves to some other station in India. But then they had to pack and move with only their personal stuff. This time it was different.

All hands were asked to pack up everything, that was NOT needed for an emergency, like war, and that meant everything. So, all decorative items, trophies, carpets, paintings, flower pots – that is, anything that made the Alfa Mess a treat to visit had to be taken away. To General Sandhu's eyes, his beloved Mess looked as if the Pakistani *kabailis* (tribals) had raided it, as they had done in Baramulla in 1947, and stripped it naked of all its beauty.

Stripping the Chinar Auditorium of its projection system, speakers, even the chairs and curtains – was heart-breaking. This was Sandhu's fifth posting in Srinagar, and in all, as he calculated silently, he would have watched at least a thousand movies in this venerable cinema hall. The fact that this was the only functioning cinema hall left in Srinagar had turned this auditorium into a congregation point for the high-and-mighty of Srinagar. That was valuable for networking, for cultivating 'sources' for military intelligence, and for obliging all and sundry who couldn't for love or money get access to any movie theatre in Srinagar. All thanks to the radical Islamists who considered it *haram* (a sin) to watch any moving pictures.

Is it a good idea to send all non-combatants before dawn broke? Officers debated in hushed tones. General Sandhu was not sure. The SOP about not moving before dawn and after dusk had a logic that hundreds of army casualties had established over decades of experience in conducting operations in the dreaded Kashmir Valley. You don't move when you can't see the enemy. Period.

Unless you knew where the enemy was holed up and you had the task to smoke them out.

But this time, it was NOT about any army operation. It was about saving money. And cutting losses. And so, it looked like the army auditors, those 'bloody civilian bean-counters' were winning. And why won't they, when they had the full support of those dhotiwala politicians, General Sandhu sighed.

Just then, a bark broke his reverie.

Bhojan taiyar hai Shriman.

Ah, that was the Mess Havildar announcing that the dinner was ready.

The good General nodded and motioned his colleagues to move to the High Table. The Divisional Commissioner (DivCom), Kashmir and the Inspector General of Police (IGP), Kashmir were also attending. Both 'gentlemen' were drunk till their gills, despite being devout Kashmiri Muslims. They were obviously going beyond their Holy Book to imbibe the good whiskey of the infidels, General Sandhu surmised.

Even in their stupor, the civilian officers couldn't help but notice the stripped look of the Alfa Mess.

"What is happening? Is the GOC under transfer," whispered Noor Khan the IGP.

"Huh?" grunted Tufail Chattoo, the DivCom.

"You know, when these Army generals get transferred, they take away all the good stuff of their messes with their personal baggage. Just as our ministers do ... to their official residences when they lose elections?" winked the IGP.

"Hey, but this GOC came only six months back," remembered the DivCom, "and the GOCs generally have a tenure of at least two years in the Corps."

"Unless they are retiring or are being kicked up in promotion," argued the IGP.

"Sir, the dinner is laid," the ADC to GOC approached the civilian officers and escorted them to their seats at the far end of the High Table, beyond where the Brigadiers were seated. Under the civilian Warrant of Precedence, the divisional level officers may have the rank of a Lt General, but the Indian Army following the pre-independence practice was keeping them two rungs below, at the level of Brigadiers.

As the officers took their seats at the High Table, everyone else queued up for the buffet, more or less in accordance with their rank. Liveried waiters scurried around the High Table unfolding the starch-stiff napkins and offering them to the dignitaries to place them on their laps. General Sandhu, however, stuck his napkin loosely under his shirt collar.

"That's what you do for babies," Noor Khan whispered.

"Sh...h...h..." Tufail motioned to his irreverent junior colleague.

As the band played in the background, the first course was served.

"Not vegetarian almond soup again," Noor Khan shuddered. Like most Kashmiris, he hated everything that was vegetarian. Or grown in Kashmir.

And it was almond soup. Once again!

Then some appetisers were served. Small pieces of mutton kebab, fried chicken nuggets, *hara-bhara kababs* and fried *idlis* – the standard fare. The civilian officers asked for the vegetarian options as they couldn't as Muslims eat any non-vegetarian dish that was not made with halal meat.

At least not in public.

As the entrée dishes were replaced by full dinner plates, the main course was served one by one. Gushtabba (the meatball cooked in a white yoghurt curry), Butter Chicken or Chicken Makhni, Paneer-Matar (cottage cheese with peas), cauliflower-potato, broccoli in white sauce, Rajma (kidney bean) curry, and four other vegetarian dishes that most guests ignored. Finally, there was vegetable pulao and assorted Indian breads like naans, missi, and tandoori rotis.

Gushtabba was the only non-vegetarian item that the Kashmiri officers would accept, because they knew this was bought from the local market where they were sure to have been made with halal meat. But even that one dish was enough to rekindle the curiosity of the IGP.

"So, Brigadier Saheb, are you guys moving out to some other place?" Noor Khan asked.

"Yes," the Brigadier smirked. "To Pathankot. Kashmir is so peaceful now that I'm sure the police can very well manage things here on their own."

Year 2022

43

Srinagar, 1 January 2022

PYARE Lal Ganju woke up with a start. At 70, he was a light sleeper in any case, but this growling sound was too unsettling.

He looked at his alarm clock. It was barely 4 in the morning. All of Kashmir would be fast asleep snuggled in layers of blankets and *rajais* (quilts). *And here I'm imagining growls in this dead of winter, in the severest Chillai Kalan of all times.*

It would be two hours later, at 6 AM, when his alarm clock could go off and when Ganju would drag himself up from his warm bed. He would then move to his makeshift kitchen next to his room and make himself some Kashmiri *Noon Chai* or salted tea. Doctors had warned him about the salt in the tea being bad for his blood pressure, but they be damned.

In his sunset years, Ganju couldn't countenance switching over to 'Lipton Tea', that sweet tea that today's Kashmir was more addicted to than the *Noon Chai* that people of Ganju's generation just wouldn't give up. Of course, you could make this so-called 'Lipton Tea' with all kinds of dust tea that the brand 'Lipton' had no relation with, but the young didn't know, or care, smirked Ganju.

Half-an-hour later, around 0630 hrs, Ganju would saunter to the nearby Sonwar Temple on the banks of the River Jhelum. There to the horror of the 'outsider' devotees, he would keep out his *kangri* (the Kashmiri clay pot carrying charcoal ambers that you carry under your shapeless Kashmiri woollen pheran), strip down to his underpants, and take a dip in the freezing water of the languorously flowing river.

While in water, he would pray to the still non-existent sun god with folded hands and offer water. He would then get out, dry himself with a towel, don his clothes, take his *kangri* inside his pheran, and go around, doing a *parikrama* of all the gods and goddesses of that little temple.

And come hell or high water, Ganju had been doing this regularly for the last 30 years. Especially since 1990 when most of his Kashmiri Pandit relatives were chased away from the Valley by Islamist terrorists.

Ganju's family owned a small stationery shop in Sonwar in the sprawling 1,500-acre Badami Bagh Army Cantonment area. So, they were safe from the terrorists, they were told. But the rattled Ganjus had since then become overtly religious. And Pyare Lal was simply keeping up the tradition of taking a dip in the Jhelum every morning that his father and grandfather used to perform every day when they were in Srinagar.

Getting up to inspect the source of that growling sound at 4 in the morning was, therefore, annoying, to say the least. But in a Kashmir, overrun by Islamist zealots, you couldn't take these things lightly, could you?

So, a reluctant Pyare Lal put on his *pheran* and walked to his window on the first floor of his house. Bracing himself, he opened the windows and stuck his neck out to have a better look. The cold winds stung his cheeks like a knife carved out from snow. But it was the sight below that took his breath away.

The growl was actually a rumble he could now hear clearly. Coming out from hundreds of *Shaktimaans,* the formidable army trucks, creeping out of the main gate of the Badami Bagh Army Cantonment. Yes, *creeping* because they were moving out at the speed of a bare twenty kilometres an hour! Using their parking lights, and NOT their headlights on high beam as they usually do. Which gave an impression they were sneaking out on some secret mission.

Ma Sharda, a prayer escaped Ganju's lips. Are we heading for a war? With Pakistan? Or China?

Don't be stupid, you *Batta.* Pyare Lal used the same pejorative term for himself that the majority Kashmiri Muslims were fond of using for Kashmiri Pandits, the miniscule minority. It is January, and you don't fight wars with Pakistan or China on the J&K (Jammu and Kashmir) front in winters.

Also, the convoy was heading south, towards Banihal, and Jammu. Not north towards Baramulla or the POK (Pak-Occupied Kashmir). So, there was no war on the horizon. Definitely. Ganju slapped himself, closed the windows, and turned to his bed.

And then from the corner of his eyes, he noticed a break in the pattern. After some twenty *Shaktimaans*, were sneaking out some ten *Ashok Leyland* buses. And they all contained people in civvies – army wives, children, and non-combatants like gardeners, helpers, etc, Ganju surmised.

But why are the non-combatants being moved out, so surreptitiously, and before daylight broke? This was against all army SOPs (Standard Operating Procedures) that Ganju knew of – that mandated army convoy movement only from dawn-to-dusk.

Is Indian Army abandoning Kashmir?

Pyare Lal slapped himself again at this foolish thought and went back to sleep.

44

Awantipora, 1 January 2022

GANJU was not the only one who had noticed the gigantic army convoy moving out of Srinagar at that unearthly hour. The dozing sentry at the Pantha Chowk Police Station was the next. He used his wireless set to inform his SHO (Station House Officer), who passed on the message to the District SP (Superintendent of Police). The SP in turn alerted the Police Control Room. Thereafter every police station from Srinagar to Qazigund was crackling with messages, conjectures, and commentaries about this 'unusual' move of the army convoy.

Abu Farzana, the Pak-backed Kashmir chief of Lashkar-e-Toiba (LeT), was fast asleep in his hide-out in Pampore, the saffron town of Kashmir, when the police wireless set, that he had snatched only a day back from a policeman, burst to life. Farzana woke up with a start. *Ah, Allah be praised.* So, the policeman had still not reported the 'theft' of his wireless set as that would have surely led to the change of the wireless frequencies that the JK Police used.

As Farzana made sense of the messages being exchanged, his eyes squinted and his face widened in disbelief. Just then, he heard the rumbling sounds and realised that the convoy was almost upon his location. Nothing could now be done in Pampore, but Farzana was not going to give up so easily.

Farzana rang up his associate in Awantipora. "Bashir? Are you awake?"

"Now, I am," an irritated Bashir retorted.

"Listen, in about half-an-hour, an army convoy would be reaching your place. There are some buses in between – full of women and children – that should be easy to attack. Can you rig up a small IED (Incendiary Explosive Device) on the road in front of the Awantipora ruins where such convoys always slow down to gawk and blow up a nice bus to smithereens?"

"Farzana, I haven't even said my prayers as yet. And are you sure the convoy doesn't have mine-sweeping vehicles?"

"Bashir, killing infidels is the best prayer to Allah and you are sure to be rewarded for that noble deed. So just get out and carry out Allah's command."

"Okay," Bashir replied. Reluctance in his tone. The call over, he went to his almirah and took out two fully assembled IEDs. Bashir debated whether he should fit them with pressure switches so that they detonate the moment a heavy vehicle goes over them. This was safer as he need not then be close by.

Or, he could link them to a mobile phone and trigger them by calling up that number. But then, he had to supervise this operation personally which was riskier.

But the latter operation had a better chance of hitting the right target. Plus, when you have chosen to be a *mujahedeen* (holy warrior), you can't fear death. Earth for you is just a 'transit station'. And it is the afterlife with the promise of those 72 *hoories* or fairies in heaven that spur all your actions.

Bashir sprinted to the National Highway 1, located the small speed breaker in front of the ruins, and placed an IED each on both ends. Earlier on one of his reconnaissance missions, he had hollowed out portions at both ends of the speed breaker so that when the need arises, he could place an IED there and cover that with rubble.

Job done. Bashir hid himself behind a bush some fifty metres away and waited.

Fifteen minutes later the convoy was reaching him. The headlights were on and the high beams were blinding in their intensity. The diesel fumes, as they hung just above the road in that cold air, reduced the visibility of a misty winter morning even further.

Bashir found it difficult to breathe. But what compounded his discomfort was the decision: of when to trigger the explosive device.

The escort vehicle, full with armed-to-the-teeth soldiers, was the first to arrive. Bashir waited as he knew this could be an armoured vehicle. And it was.

Plus, Bashir had to target the women and children bus as that contained the maximum number of infidels. There was an additional advantage. Whenever such an attack happened, the army soldiers would go berserk ransacking nearby villages and beating up everyone who came their way. That created good publicity for the cause and almost always resulted in an avalanche of visits from do-gooders – the human rights activists, the peaceniks, the secular brigade, the Lutyens media, even an odd official from the UN – which was all fantastic.

Bashir pressed the number for the first IED and was ready to dial. After the first two escort vehicles, the *Shaktiman* trucks went over the speed breaker one by one. He squinted as he counted twenty trucks before he could notice the outline of what he thought could be the first Ashok Leyland bus.

Bashir waited till he was sure that this bus contained women and other non-combatants. Now was the time to display his artistry.

He pressed the call key just as the second bus was going over the hump. The ringing sound started on Bashir's mobile, but the rings continued till they were terminated with that irritating recording that declared, "*The number you are calling is either switched off or not answering.*"

Bashir quickly dialled the number of the other IED. The result was the same.

Damn. Is the network down?

Bashir looked at the signal level on his mobile. It showed three bars which was not bad.

Ah, could it be then that the battery of the mobiles attached to the IEDs were discharged? But Bashir remembered having a look at them when he had switched them on about half-an-hour back. And they were about 60% full.

And then it struck Bashir. The bastards were using jammers! For the entire convoy?

Bashir had learnt in his training camp in Muzaffarabad in 'Azad Kashmir', (that the Indians called 'Pak-Occupied Kashmir' or POK) that jammers were expensive devices that the Indians could afford to use only for their VVIPs. So, what happened here?

Bashir had heard rumours about how thick the Indians had become with the Israelis lately. Could it be that they had supplied some cheap but nifty jamming devices that this entire convoy was able to use? Was that why this convoy had moved so early in the morning without waiting for the usual ROPs (Road Opening Parties) to check and sanitise the entire National Highway?

He had to get back to Farzana immediately. But the convoy was still passing by Bashir's position.

Bashir composed a quick SMS. "Bhai, mission failed. Bastards r using jammers I think."

Bashir was startled when his mobile rang. So, the jammers are gone! It was Farzana on the other side.

"Bashir, how can you botch up this simple operation? I was counting on you so much...."

Bashir whispered back his explanations. Farzana was unconvinced. He suspected that Bashir had not even got out of his house and was fobbing. He was questioning and Bashir was explaining.

In the spate of arguments and counter-arguments that were following one-another, Bashir failed to notice the tiny whirr of the *Prahari* (Sentinel) drone that suddenly came out of nowhere and was now hovering about thirty feet above Bashir.

A special unit in the Drone Management Vehicle (DMV) at the tail end of the convoy was monitoring the images transmitted by the ten drones flying over the convoy on both sides. When an agitated Bashir explaining his operation looked up for a moment, the drone captured his face and relayed the image. The computer bank analysed the image in the blink of an eye and informed the CO (Commanding Officer) that this was no ordinary villager answering the nature's call in the open. This was Bashir, ace IED expert of the LeT, and close associate of the dreaded Abu Farzana.

The rat-a-tat gunfire caught Bashir totally by surprise. A drone fired at him non-stop. Bashir was dead even before his body slumped to the ground. On the open line on Bashir's mobile, Farzana heard Bashir's shrieks, and the sound of gun fire.

Farzana wondered if his instructions to Bashir were leaked out by a mole in his unit. But that will be a task he will have to tackle later. Right now, he had to activate his Bijbehara unit and then the Qazigund unit to attack the army convoy. There was no way Farzana was going to accept defeat.

Not yet. Not so easily.

45

Qazigund, 1 January 2022

"WHERE were you, you bastard," Farzana shouted and added a few choicest abuses when Ahmed finally picked up his call.

"Of course, praying Farzana Bhai. What else do you expect me to do at seven in the morning?... And if you are bothered about Taploo, that Kashmiri Pandit, who I have to dispatch today, then don't worry. My plans are ready, and there is no way Taploo is going to see his *Surya Bagwan* (the sun god) tomorrow."

"Taploo my foot," Farzana exploded. "Forget that bastard because I've a bigger assignment for you today."

"Huh," Ahmed exclaimed, "I'm listening."

Farzana barked. "There is a huge army convoy coming your way anytime now. There are some ten buses carrying women, children, and some unarmed personnel. Earlier, I had asked Bashir to take care of them but he has goofed up. Big time. So, I'm asking you to handle this. All right?"

"Okay, Farzana Bhai. But as you say there may not be any time to lay anything on the road. I also see the ROPs sweeping for mines right in front of the house I'm in. So as an experienced senior, could you tell me what exactly you want me to do?"

"Why should I be doing all your thinking for you?" shouted Farzana.

"Okay, I could then gather a crowd of twenty boys, which would ... hmm ... cost me at 1,000 per head ... ₹ 20,000, to throw stones at the convoy. Four of them, at ₹ 3,000 per head, will throw some hand grenades and scoot. Will that do?"

"Ahmed, you fool, why can't you get my point?" Farzana was still furious. "I want to inflict maximum damage on this convoy, and that's all. So, get on to the highest point on the route with a bazooka and blast a few buses sky high."

"But Farzana Bhai," Ahmed argued back, "that would mean my immediate *shahadat* (martyrdom) today. I had a few errands to run before I do that."

"Ahmed, my little brother," Farzana's tone suddenly became all sugar-and-honey. "You know, how much Allah loves you. And how much would He like you to be with Him soon? So just SMS me the errands you wanted to run today and I'll personally take care of them all.

"But remember, you don't get such chances of ascending to heaven every day. You have the opportunity to kill hundreds of Hindu infidels today, and you will be a fool to let such a chance escape your hands. Ah, just think of the juicy dates, and the river of wine awaiting you in heaven. And those 72 ample-bosomed *hoories* (fairies). Hasn't your *Murshid* (teacher) told you about these just rewards?"

Ahmed was a little hesitant. Time was not on his side, but he knew of the building in Qazigund from where he could launch this attack. It was also easy to escape from that building into the labyrinthine streets of the town. Ahmed was in no hurry to meet his *hoories* but arguing any further with Farzana was futile. Any attempt to defy him would result in unthinkable retribution, on him, and on his young wife and kid, in the nearby village.

"Okay, Farzana Bhai," Ahmed sighed, "Don't worry. I'll carry out the attack as you desire. And hopefully, the number of infidels I'll send to hell today will ensure mine and yours position in heaven forever. Bye, then. And see you soon, Insha'Allah (God willing)."

"That's my *mujaheedin* (soldier of Islam)," Farzana declared and disconnected the call.

Ahmed called up Basharat, his associate, and both called up their contacts in Bijbehara, and other small towns on the route. Soon they had a fairly good idea of when the convoy would reach the kill zone in Qazigund.

Both then picked up their bazookas with ammunition. They also tied their small arms with magazines around their waists. From their experience, they knew that after their *mission* was over, these small arms could only help in their escape.

Then they picked up their back-packs, put a packet each of dates, almonds, and dried figs inside, attached their water bottle, and started their journey towards the highest house they had planned to occupy.

Qazigund was yet to wake up fully on that misty winter morning. But whosoever they encountered on the way scampered away at the sight of those heavy bazookas they were carrying.

After about ten minutes of brisk walking, Ahmed and Basharat had reached the target house. Ahmed knocked on the door aggressively.

"*Kussa chhu*?" Who is this? A voice asked in Kashmiri as the lady of the house opened the door. Ahmed rushed in and almost knocked the lady down. Basharat sauntered in and closed the door behind.

The lady whimpered with fear.

"Look *Khala* (aunt)," Ahmed addressed the woman in chaste Kashmiri. "We are not here to hurt anyone. Unless you create a racket. So, gather your wits and round up every one."

The lady rushed around the house and woke up everyone. Soon there was a motley crowd, of some ten souls, wearing varying shades of *pheran* (Kashmiri loose woollen gown), and standing around the gunmen. There were a few good-looking females that looked interesting. But they will have to await their good fortune of serving a *mujaheedin*, Ahmed shook his head.

"Come on, all of you, get inside this room, cover yourselves with blankets if you feel cold, but regardless of what happens, don't make a sound. Understood?" Ahmed barked.

Basharat used the butt of his gun to shoo everyone in. Then he bolted the door from the outside and with Ahmed made his way to the roof of the house. There were faint sobbing sounds coming from the locked room, but the duo couldn't care less.

The attic was full of junk – broken furniture, old newspapers, grandfather's radio from the 1970s.... Ahmed pushed some aside and climbed over some other to reach the window. That dislodged a lot of dust that had Basharat, who was following behind, suffering a bout of coughing and sneezing.

"You Kashmiri Sissie," Ahmed sniggered, "and you want to be a *mujaheedin*!"

Basharat took out a hankie from his *pheran* and tied on his face. By the time he had reached the window, Ahmed was standing on the ledge and was looking for something to hoist him up the sloping GI (galvanised iron) roof. Soon he found the railing that Kashmiris use to help them clean snow from their roofs and pulled at it to check its strength. Satisfied, he handed over his weapons to Basharat and climbed up.

Ahmed sat down with his legs resting on the railing, and asked Basharat to pass on the weapons. That done, he bent down to lend a helping hand to Basharat and pulled him up.

It was time they reported their readiness to Farzana, their Supreme Commander.

Farzana picked up the call at the first ring. "Ahmed, where are you now?"

"Bhai, I and Basharat are in position."

"And what about others?"

"Others? Bhai, we thought we two *Ghazis* (Muslim warriors fighting infidels) are enough to dispatch hundreds of Hindu *kafirs* to their hell," a puzzled Ahmed replied.

"Since when have you started thinking, Ahmed? I had asked you to make fool proof arrangements to target this huge army convoy, and you come up with a two-man plan?"

"Farzana Bhai, don't worry. I'm asking Faquir and Qadri too to take up a position on the other side of the road two hundred metres ahead of us on the Srinagar side."

"Good and keep me posted about the operation. Ring me up before you fire the first shot and keep the line open."

Ahmed rang up Faquir while Basharat woke up Qadri. There were a lot of arguments and counter-arguments, where after it was settled that Faquir and Qadir too will join the holy war at the site settled between them.

Half-an-hour later, Qadir rang up to confirm they too were in position. Now where was the blasted convoy?

Ahmed's mobile vibrated to show a text message had arrived. It was Farzana. It read,

"Convoy delayed. Drivers having tea at Khanabal army camp. Expect action by 0845."

Ahmed forwarded the message to Faquir, and now both parties waited.

At 0840 hrs, Ahmed heard a helicopter. Faquir and Qadir too heard it and craned their necks to spot the flying machine. Helicopters were a common sight in Kashmir. There were army Cheetahs and Chetaks, and Bells and Eurocopters of the State Government. And then there were those Pawan Hans choppers flying pilgrims for Amarnath.

Suddenly, about a kilometre away, two Mi-17 gunship helicopters emerged from the top of the Poplar trees. And before Ahmed realised, he saw them raining bullets below.

On the open line, Ahmed heard shrieks and swear words as someone was hit. Badly. And then it struck Ahmed. The Mi-17s had just gunned down Faquir and Qadir and were now coming for him.

"Basharat run-n-n-n-n," Ahmed shouted as he slithered down the roof.

Ahmed nicked his palms at the rusted nails that were keeping the roof in place. He reached the window and swung down to the attic.

Basharat in panic had picked up the bazooka and was trying to come down using his other hand. In the process, he slipped.

"Eeeeeee," Basharat shrieked as he fell two stories down in the kitchen garden.

As Ahmed watched in horror, Basharat's body lay motionless in a grotesque heap on the ground. But there was no time to lose. The blasted Mi-17s were now coming towards him.

Ahmed scampered down the stairs, went to the ground floor room where he had locked up the family members, and flung open the bolts. "Run-n-n-n ... run outside. Army helicopters are attacking this house."

As bewildered Kashmiris, of all shapes and sizes, rushed outside the house, shrieking, "*Ya Allah, mujhe bacha le.*" O God, save our souls. Ahmed joined them.

* * *

Wing Commander Joshi piloting the helicopter had spotted the two terrorists with what looked like bazookas in their hands precariously perched on the sloping roof of a big Kashmiri house. And he was flying straight to *neutralise* them.

Oh. Oh. Looks like our action on those two terrorists a few second back has alerted these bastards, Joshi muttered under his breath as he found the two terrorists slipping and tumbling down the roof. One fellow fell straight to the ground while the other had disappeared, inside the building.

Joshi had half a mind to blast the house to smithereens when he saw at least ten civilians rushing out of the building. Some were waving their arms as if to plead they be not shot at.

Wing Commander Joshi restrained himself and radioed the location of the house to his base. They will now liaise with the local army and police units and try to catch and neutralise those terrorists. His job done, Joshi turned to the National Highway 1-A to escort the army convoy, which was his main task for the day.

Half an hour later, the convoy would cross the Banihal tunnel into Jammu where after Joshi would return to his base at Awantipora Station of the Indian Air Force.

* * *

SP Sunil Jalla of the Mobile Tower Unit was tracing the calls of Abu Farzana from the time he had dared to abduct the State's Chief Secretary. The orders had come from the DGP, who

Sunil learnt was under tremendous pressure from the Governor – to deliver Farzana, dead or alive, or else!

Normally tracing an experienced terrorist like Farzana was a difficult task as Farzana was wont to use a different sim for different calls. That meant using on an average twenty numbers for twenty different calls, every day. But today, Farzana was angry for some reason. And careless. He had made three five minutes or longer calls and hadn't bothered to change either his sim or his location.

Jalla called Major Paramjit Singh, his counterpart in the Rashtriya Rifles unit that was closest to Farzana, "Major Saheb, are you ready to scalp a good mujaheedin today?"

"*Are* Sunil Sir, *yeh bhi koi poochne ki baat hai?* Tell me, who is this … this time?"

"Abu Farzana. He's also the one trying to coordinate the attack on the army convoy today."

"And where is that bastard hiding?" Major Singh was seething, but excited.

"In Pulwama, I'm just sending his co-ordinates," said Sunil as he texted the details.

* * *

Abu Farzana had been speaking to Ahmed when the sound of running feet startled him. He gazed through the window and saw that men in military camouflage uniforms had surrounded the house he was in. Abu Farzana looked up in the air. *Looks like, my time has come,* he muttered.

He picked up his AK-47 and fired a few shots at the soldiers. The soldiers fired back and the gun battle continued for a few hours. Acrid smoke from the shells fired by the soldiers stung Farzana's eyes.

Suddenly, a blast blew off the doors of Farzana's room. As he swung around in surprise, Major Singh fired a volley at him.

As the bullets pierced Farzana's chest and abdomen, he tumbled backwards and fell on the ground.

His breathing heavy, he prayed to Allah for one final time hoping to enter his paradise. But no vision of dates, or rivers of wine, or those *hoories* came to his eyes. He was in terrible pain and could hardly see anything. Till his heart stopped and his eyes turned lifeless.

46

Qazigund, 1 April 2022

MOBASSHIR was stuck in this huge traffic jam just beyond Qazigund at the point where the road ascended towards the Banihal tunnel. He was going to Jammu's Narwal Fruit Mandi to collect the money that was due to him from the trader who had taken some three hundred cartons of apples from him a month back. Don't ask why the trader couldn't remit the money to Mobasshir electronically because in J&K – regardless of what Government of India wished – cash was still king.

Mobasshir grew impatient. The traffic jam was unusual. Had some truck toppled on the way blocking traffic? No one knew.

Could there be a police or army operation underway to eliminate some 'terrorists' who Kashmiris call 'militants'? But Mobasshir couldn't hear any of those familiar gunshots.

"Route clearance for Amarnath Yatris?" But that yatra was to start from 14 June, wasn't it?

The suspense was killing. So Mobasshir got out to investigate. Yes, the place was swarming with uniforms, just ahead of the traffic jam. What looked like was that they were checking papers and only occasionally letting a vehicle move.

"I think they are allowing only officials to go up the tunnel today," a man surmised who had two kids in his Maruti. "I was taking them to a National selection camp for Wushu, but I don't know when we will reach Jammu," he added.

Mobasshir didn't know what to say.

Suddenly, he heard a rumble, of road-crunching heavy traffic, coming his way. As he stopped in his tracks to investigate, he was joined in by a jostling crowd of over a thousand irate Kashmiris. The oncoming traffic appeared to be driving only half on tarmac because there was so much dust all-around.

As the roar came closer, and the dust clouds parted, the onlookers gasped. This was a fifty-long convoy of Arjun main battle tanks of the Indian Army chugging at a sedate speed of forty kilometres or so an hour. Every tank had two soldiers in uniform looking out menacingly. The tanks were so huge that they couldn't fit on whatever was left of the roads. That's why they were half on the tarmac and half outside.

"Has a war broken out? With Pakistan?" someone muttered in Kashmiri.

But shouldn't they be going the other way then, towards Muzaffarabad? Mobasshir wondered.

"Unless war has broken out in Jammu," a third driver said aloud.

That did it!

Kashmiris in panic started their vehicles, reversed, and sped back to Kashmir, as far away from Banihal as they could manage.

The soldiers manning the barriers noticed the thinning of vehicles and couldn't help but let out a smile. This was so easy after all.

Now they just had to focus on their tanks, and other heavy armour that was following them, to make their way to Banihal before night fall.

And seal the tunnel thereafter.

Epilogue
D + 1 Day

KASHMIR CELEBRATIONS, 2 APRIL 2022

Whole night there were drum beats in the streets of Srinagar celebrating 'the retreat of the Indian infidels'. People initially thought it was a rumour, but the Indian Prime Minister's speech at the UN General Assembly at around 1100 hrs in New York (and around 9 PM in Srinagar) confirmed it all. Among many other things, in which he had underlined the greatness of the Indian civilisation, he said:

> *In the Comity of nations, India has a special place of honour ... because it not only preaches but also practices its policy of vasudhaiva kutumbakam or the entire world is my family. For millennia, India's doors have been open to people of all faiths, races, cultures, languages ... so much so that every persecuted faith – be it the Zoroastrian Parsees, Bahais, Ahmedias, Bohras, Syrian Christians, or all the 72 sects of Islam, everyone is today happily living and thriving in India. That open-door policy is*

now reciprocated by almost all our neighbours, and many more, with the result that today Indians have visa-free access to over 100 countries.

India has never coveted anyone's land. And so, we are hurt when we are accused by an intransigent neighbour of occupying a Valley, which we thought was always ours. A region that was the crown of India from the time the great Emperor Ashok founded the city of Srinagar, from the time Panini, Patanjali, and Abhinav Gupt completed their seminal works in this beautiful region, and from where the legendary King Lalitaditya extended his empire from the Caspian Sea in the west to Assam in the east and the Kaveri basin in the south. Unfortunately for us, that Valley too thinks that India has been discriminatory, cruel, and callous to them and to their sentiments and aspirations.

So, a mature India, which is fiercely proud of its secular credentials, has decided to let this Valley go its own way. Ladies and Gentlemen of the United Nations, that Valley is Kashmir and today India makes history by honouring unilaterally, and with no pressure from any quarter, the Security Council Resolution 47, adopted on April 21, 1948, by removing all its forces, and everyone who is a non-Kashmiri from that Valley and grants Kashmir its FREEDOM. It is now for the UN to prevail upon Pakistan to similarly withdraw all its nationals from Kashmir which was always the first step and which never happened. Thereafter, the UN shall be free to initiate the third step of nominating a plebiscite administrator to conduct a free and impartial plebiscite.

I wish Kashmir well. May the Almighty show them the path where they will be much happier than when they were allegedly forced to be with India.

People rushed to the cantonment areas: in Srinagar, Pattan, Baramulla, Uri, Tangdhar, Gulmarg to re-confirm. It was eerily silent everywhere. There was indeed not a single Indian soldier to be seen anywhere.

People wanted to loot, pillage, burn, demolish, but the cantonment areas were soon swarming with Kashmiri policemen who claimed they had been ordered to take over all those properties. CM Hasina Ittoo came on radio and TV to claim credit for getting *Azaadi* and appealed to maintain order. She announced that all military areas hitherto occupied by the Indian Army would now be housing colleges and universities.

"Kashmir is finally de-militarised, and we will soon convert all swords into ploughshares," she announced grandiosely.

"Friends of Kashmir," a coalition hastily put together by some Delhi-based lawyers and journalists moved the Supreme Court of India claiming that this move to grant independence to Kashmir was illegal and unconstitutional as no provision of the Indian Constitution permitted secession. India was supposedly "an indestructible Union of States," they claimed.

Hurriyat announced 'Muzaffarabad Chalo' – a plan to march to 'Azad Kashmir' the next day but were told by their Pakistani handlers to hold their horses. The *Pakis* wanted to ensure that there were no Indian agents in the procession, they explained.

There were reports of a reverse procession, however. Of tribals from Azad Kashmir who were 'dying to unite' with their kinsmen in the 'Indian-occupied Kashmir', who till recently were suffering so badly under the jackboots of the Indian oppressors.

"Like the *kabayalis* of 1947?" an octogenarian queried who had witnessed first-hand how their so-called liberators from Pakistan had raped and plundered Baramulla then.

"Shhh ... things would be much different now," said an irritated relative who didn't want that stale history to come in the way of their celebrations.

[To be continued ...]